DILEMMAS, CHALLENGES,
AND ETHICS OF HUMANITARIAN ACTION

Dilemmas, Challenges, and Ethics of Humanitarian Action

Reflections on Médecins Sans Frontières' Perception Project

Edited by

CAROLINE ABU-SADA

Published for Médecins Sans Frontières
by
McGill-Queen's University Press
Montreal & Kingston • London • Ithaca

© McGill-Queen's University Press 2012

ISBN 978-0-7735-4085-9 (cloth)
ISBN 978-0-7735-4086-6 (paper)

Legal deposit fourth quarter 2012
Bibliothèque nationale du Québec

Printed in Canada on acid-free paper that is 100% ancient forest free
(100% post-consumer recycled), processed chlorine free

McGill-Queen's University Press acknowledges the support of the Canada
Council for the Arts for our publishing program. We also acknowledge
the financial support of the Government of Canada through the Canada
Book Fund for our publishing activities.

Library and Archives Canada Cataloguing in Publication

Dilemmas, challenges, and ethics of humanitarian action:
reflections on Médecins Sans Frontières' Perception Project /
edited by Caroline Abu-Sada.

Based on papers presented at the MSF Perceptions Conference
held in Montréal, Québec on Feb. 11, 2011.
Includes bibliographical references and index.
ISBN 978-0-7735-4085-9 (bound). – ISBN 978-0-7735-4086-6 (pbk.)

1. Doctors Without Borders (Association). 2. Doctors Without
Borders (Association) – Public opinion. 3. Humanitarian assistance –
Political aspects. 4. Humanitarian assistance – Moral and ethical
aspects. 5. Disaster medicine – Political aspects. 6. Disaster
medicine – Moral and ethical aspects. I. Abu-Sada, Caroline, 1979–
II. Médecins sans frontières (Association)

RA390.A2D54 2012   610'.601   C2012-904393-1

This book was typeset by Interscript in 10/13 Sabon.

Contents

Acronyms   vii

Introduction   3
Caroline Abu-Sada

PART 1: PERCEPTION OF MSF AS AN ORGANIZATION

1 Reversing the Optics: MSF's Perception Project   11
Caroline Abu-Sada and Khurshida Mambetova

2 At the Limits of Perception: Humanitarian Principles
in Action   29
François Cooren and Frédérik Matte

3 The Nigerian Lead-poisoning Epidemic: The Role
of Neoliberal Globalization and the Challenges
for Humanitarian Ethics   48
John D. Pringle and Donald C. Cole

PART 2: PERCEPTION OF THE CHALLENGES FACED
BY HUMANITARIAN ACTORS

4 Western Clinical Health Ethics: How Well Do They Travel
to Humanitarian Contexts?   73
*Lisa Schwartz, Matthew Hunt, Chris Sinding, Laurie Elit,
Lynda Redwood-Campbell, Naomi Adelson, Sonya De Laat,
and Jennifer Ranford*

5 Programming, Footprints, and Relationships:
   The Link between Perceptions and Humanitarian Security 89
   Larissa Fast

6 Professionalizing Humanitarian Action   104
   Kirsten Johnson

   Conclusion: The Shape of Things to Come – An Essay on
   Humanitarian Challenges   116
   Peter Walker

   MSF Charter   123

   Contributors   125

   Index   135

Acronyms

ACEP	American College of Emergency Physicians
ALNAP	Active Learning Network for Accountability and Performance in Humanitarian Action
AMA	American Medical Association
BCE	Before the Common Era
CBHA	Consortium of British Humanitarian Agencies
CDC	Centers for Disease Control and Prevention
CE	Common Era
CIHR	Canadian Institutes of Health Research
CLANSM	Collaborative Learning Approach to NGO Security Management
ECB	Emergency Capacity Building Project
ELRHA	Enhancing Learning and Research for Humanitarian Assistance
ED	Emergency Department
EM	Emergency Medicine
GDP	gross domestic product
HAP-I	Humanitarian Accountability Partnership International
HELP	Humanitarian and Emergency Logistics Professionals
HIV/AIDS	Human Immunodeficiency Virus/Acquired Immunodeficiency Syndrome
HPN	Humanitarian Practice Network
IASC	Inter-Agency Standing Committee

ICRC	International Committee of the Red Cross
IDP	Internally Displaced People
IMF	International Monetary Fund
INEE	Inter-Agency Network for Education in Emergencies
INGO	International Non-Governmental Organization
LEGS	Livestock Emergency Guidelines and Standard
MINURCAT	United Nations Mission in the Central African Republic and Chad
MOH	Ministry of Health
MSF	Médecins Sans Frontières
MSF-CH	Swiss section of Médecins Sans Frontières
NOHA	Network of Humanitarian Assistance
NGO	Non-Governmental Organization
ODI	Overseas Development Institute
OPEC	Organization of Petroleum Exporting Countries
PHAP	Professionals in Humanitarian Assistance and Protection
SUD	Coordination Solidarité, Urgence, Développement
TB	tuberculosis
UN	United Nations
UNESCO	United Nations Education, Scientific and Cultural Organization
UNFPA	United Nations Population Fund
UK	United Kingdom
URD	Groupe Urgence, Réhabilitation, Développement
US	United States
VDF	Village des Femmes
WB	World Bank
WHO	World Health Organization
WTO	World Trade Organization

DILEMMAS, CHALLENGES,
AND ETHICS OF HUMANITARIAN ACTION

Introduction

The way humanitarian actors are perceived has attracted increased attention in recent years, mainly because of the emergence of new actors who challenge the very foundations of a certain form of humanitarian action, blurring lines between humanitarian and political agendas, and supposedly resulting in growing difficulties in gaining access to populations in conflict zones.[1]

Médecins Sans Frontières/Doctors Without Borders (MSF) is a non-profit, non-governmental organization (NGO) that provides medical assistance to populations caught up in crises that threaten their survival[2] – mainly armed conflicts but also epidemics, pandemics, natural disasters, or even exclusion from health care. Created in France in 1971 by doctors and journalists, it is now an international movement made up of nineteen associations, each under the responsibility of a board of directors elected by the association members during an annual general assembly. In 1999, MSF was awarded the Nobel Peace Prize. Today, the organization provides aid in more than sixty countries and employs nearly twenty-seven thousand people.[3] However, at this point in its history, MSF considered it important to launch the Perception Project in order to give voice to the people living in the areas in which it provides medical relief.

MSF acts according to principles of independence, neutrality, and impartiality.[4] To a degree, these principles have become MSF's hallmark and have led it to refuse to collaborate with other actors or to use the infrastructures and resources deployed by other humanitarian or international organizations on the ground. Consequently, some consider it more isolationist than independent.[5] Unlike other humanitarian actors, MSF enjoys financial independence,[6] which sets it apart and now forms part of its identity. "Témoignage" is also something very specific to the organization,[7] and it was one of the main reasons for its creation. Following the Biafran War, MSF's founders wanted to create an organization that, unlike the International Committee of the Red Cross (ICRC), would speak out publicly about what it was seeing in the field and not remain silent. Forty years later, témoignage is still considered an integral part of its work.[8] However, the priority given to medical action remains firm.

MSF considers that its capacity for action, based on its independence, is threatened by the initiatives of certain states and international organizations that use humanitarian relief as a tool to achieve their political objectives. The association has, therefore, felt it necessary to distance itself from these attempts to manipulate humanitarian action by highlighting, through its communications and operations, its difference – its independence.

This publication follows a conference that was organized by MSF in Montreal on 11 February 2011. It gathered around eighty people, mostly academics, humanitarian workers, and students. Introduced by the president and the general director of MSF Canada, the conference provided a platform for discussing issues at stake in the humanitarian world today: the challenges, the dilemmas, and the ethical questions that inevitably arise from MSF's practice.

This event also took place in order to share the results of a research project conducted between 2007 and 2011 by MSF-CH – a project that tries to understand and analyze how humanitarian action in general, and MSF in particular, is perceived today by the populations within which, and for whom, such organizations work.

One of the main challenges consists of translating humanitarian principles into operational principles. As stated in *The Practical Guide to Humanitarian Law*: "Humanitarian principles must be interpreted in a practical manner within the context of relief operations, because it is respect for these principles that guarantees humanitarian organizations the right to be present on the ground in times of armed conflict, in accordance with the Geneva Conventions."[9] This definition serves as a guide during armed conflicts but is less useful in settings in which MSF is working with neglected populations and/or neglected diseases. It is worth noting that only 22 percent of MSF's interventions in 2009 were emergency/short-term interventions,[10] which shows that MSF has also made a place for itself as a provider of longer-term medical assistance.

As a medical humanitarian organization, MSF is becoming increasingly aware of its limitations; therefore, it decided to undertake this three-year exploration of "perception" in order to gain a better understanding of the way in which it is perceived in the field by a wide variety of stakeholders, with a view to optimizing how it implements its medical projects. This research project aimed to ascertain perceptions, which, by definition, are highly transient and depend as much on political context (history of colonization; previous military or humanitarian interventions; number and types of foreign actors' present; role of religious, political, economic, and military authorities; etc.)[11] as on the way the organization presents itself to the outside world.

The way a humanitarian organization is perceived depends on a whole range of diverse and varied factors that are relatively difficult to understand. Indeed, such perception is the result of both context-independent factors (e.g., the organization's activities in other parts of the world, its reputation, its visibility on the international stage, and the consistency of its principles and activities) and characteristics linked directly to the environment in which it is operating. The latter may include the way the organization implements its operations in the country, the relevance of its activities to the needs of the local people, its communication strategy, its position with regard to national political issues, or even its management of local human resources or its integration into the pre-existing social fabric.

Perception has a considerable impact on the quality of an organization's operations (as well as on the safety of both national and expatriate staff on the ground) and their beneficiaries. Consequently, NGO teams must pay special attention to the notion of perception, both in the field and at headquarters.

The authors all delivered papers at the MSF conference in Montreal, and the chapters in this volume are based on those contributions. If some of the authors have directly worked as fieldworkers with MSF (C. Abu-Sada, K. Mambetova, F. Matte, and J. Pringle), others have been involved in research projects pertaining to MSF's activities (F. Cooren, L. Schwartz, and M. Hunt) or research projects pertaining to humanitarian action (L. Fast, K. Johnson, and P. Walker).

Chapter 1, by Caroline Abu-Sada and Khurshida Mambetova, discusses the perception research project, which was the reason for the conference. It gives a broad perspective on the project and provides examples taken from the field visit that occurred in Chad in 2010. Chapter 2, by François Cooren and Frédérik Matte, uses a communication framework to analyze the daily activities of MSF. It is the result of a research project conducted by the University of Montreal, under the direction of Cooren, which follows MSF workers both in the field and at the headquarter level to try to apprehend which figures were used in the discourses and in the actions of the people and the institution. Chapter 3, by John D. Pringle and Donald C. Cole, exposes the ethical dilemmas with which medical humanitarian aid workers are confronted when the causes of their intervention are rooted in the economic system. Chapter 4, by Lisa Schwartz and her research team, draws on interview-based research that examines the ethical challenges described by humanitarian health care providers. Chapter 5, by Larissa Fast, broadly explores the way communities perceive humanitarian action and how "acceptance" has become a new security framework for some aid organizations. Chapter 6, by Kirsten Johnson, defends the idea that a system to measure humanitarian aid workers' accountability must be put in place in order to face the various challenges discussed in this book. In the conclusion, Peter Walker presents his vision of the challenges still facing humanitarian action in today's world.

These contributions reflect the different challenges humanitarian action is facing today, and they provide the reader, students, academics, and humanitarian workers with diverse points of view regarding the causes of these challenges and how they might be confronted. They do not, however, represent MSF's institutional point of view.

Geneva, November 2011
Caroline Abu-Sada, MSF

NOTES

1 Abby Stoddard, Adele Harmer, Victoria DiDomenico, *Providing Aid in Insecure Environments: 2009 Update, Trends in Violence against Aid Workers and the Operational Response* (London: Overseas Development Institute, 2009); C. Magone, M. Neuman, and F. Weissman, *Humanitarian Negotiations Revealed* (London: Hurst, 2011).

2 In this book, Médecins Sans Frontières/Doctors Without Borders will be referred to variously as "MSF," "the association," or "the organization."

3 Anne Vallaeys, *Médecins Sans Frontières: La Biographie* (Paris: Fayard, 2004).

4 See below: the Médecins Sans Frontières/Doctors Without Borders Charter.

5 This remark is mainly made by UN agencies and other Western organizations, especially since MSF officially opposed the proposed cluster approach to the aid system. See MSF International, *What Relation to the "Aid System"?* (Geneva: MSF, April 2007).

6 Eighty-one percent of its international funding came from private donors in 2009. See *2009 Activity Report.* (Geneva: MSF Switzerland, 2010), 25.

7 "Témoignage" refers to the act of publicly denouncing situations that the organization considers intolerable.

8 The French term is still used within MSF, but a reflection process has started within the movement, the idea being to adapt the term to the organization's public and institutional positioning activities.

9 Françoise Boucher-Saulnier, *The Practical Guide to Humanitarian Law*, 2nd ed. (Lanham: Rowman and Littlefield, 2007), 157.

10 MSF International, *Typology of MSF Projects* (Geneva: MSF International, 2010).

11 Caroline Abu-Sada, "La perception de MSF sur les terrains d'intervention: Le cas du Niger," *Humanitaire* 24 (2010): 46–53.

PART ONE

Perception of MSF as an Organization

Reversing the Optics: MSF's Perception Project

CAROLINE ABU-SADA

AND KHURSHIDA MAMBETOVA

INTRODUCTION

Médecins Sans Frontières (also known as Doctors Without Borders) conducted a three-year research project on how it is perceived in some ten countries in which it provides humanitarian medical aid.[1] With this study, MSF sought to obtain more information on local perceptions of its image and projects as well as to comprehend the general perception of humanitarian action in the areas in which it was involved.

MSF states that it acts according to strong principles of independence, neutrality, and impartiality. These principles are a "trademark" of its identity and proof of the adequacy and efficiency of its intervention. Strict adherence to these principles sometimes results in a lack of collaboration with other actors or in not using the facilities and means of other humanitarian or international organizations in the field. However, it is not clear whether these principles, which MSF considers to be part of its identity, are really understood (or, as a matter of fact, even known) by its partners, stakeholders in the field, and patients. Nor does MSF know what importance they actually give them.

Do local actors (partners, employees, patients, and host community) understand and interpret MSF's principles in the same way as does MSF? Is medical humanitarian action understood – as MSF would hope – as an act of human solidarity, provided by an impartial, independent, and neutral organization, without any hidden agenda? Does MSF take the necessary means to ensure that local stakeholders will know the difference between MSF and other aid or international actors? How is MSF seen and perceived in the field by the people it wants to assist? What criteria apply in the local settings to ensure the appreciation of MSF's presence and intervention?

In the beginning of the MSF perception project, the research unit set several objectives, which included, among others things, a focus on the organization's operational aspects. This focus differentiates this project from similar projects undertaken by other organizations and academic institutions (e.g., A. Donini's Humanitarian Agenda 2015).[2] The MSF research team had an obligation to provide the organization with tangible and practical recommendations for its field operations. In addition, the research had the following goals: to improve our understanding of the context (global, national, and local) of MSF missions; to gain a better understanding of how actors and individuals perceive MSF; to translate research findings into actions aimed at reinforcing organizational capacity; and to fuel MSF's reflections on humanitarian challenges.

Information was collected during semi-structured interviews, individually or in groups. The questionnaire developed for this study consisted of approximately sixty questions grouped by four major topics: (1) perception of humanitarian action (in general); (2) perception of MSF and its activities; (3) perception of a disease or health issue (e.g., HIV, rape, fistula, or TB); and (4) internal perceptions of MSF (by expatriates and national staff). On all field visits, whenever it was possible, the research team tried to work with graduate students who were working towards their master's degrees in political science, sociology, or anthropology. Working with graduate students allowed researchers to translate the MSF perception questionnaire into local languages and/or dialects, to ask questions in a manner and language comprehensible to the local population, and to collect information on the local population's perception of humanitarian action. Representatives of the MSF research team also conducted a series of interviews with a number of actors present in the field (e.g., local authorities, health authorities, charity groups, etc.). Reporting back to the respective MSF departments (e.g., operations, medical, etc.) and integrating the perception findings into their daily work was one of the challenges of this project.

Among the phenomena that limited the results of the perception research, one can mention the problem of translating the questionnaire and students' reports into numerous languages (e.g., Arabic, Russian, Pokot, Liberian English, Hausa, and Spanish). Some information was lost in translating various local languages and dialects into English. Also, it must be remembered that collected opinions reflected individual perceptions.

Based on feedback received from the field teams, the perception research was extremely useful to them. At the same time, it must be remembered that each report is only a snapshot of perceptions at a specific time and in a specific context. For this reason, in order to get some distance from specific contexts, researchers conducted an analysis of the common tendencies of perceptions at both regional and global levels.

MAIN RESULTS OF THE RESEARCH

Perception of MSF as an Organization

First of all, the quality of the medical care provided by MSF was clearly recognized, even if it did not always correspond to what people identified as their needs. However, the research findings suggest that most of the interviewees did not directly link the acronym "MSF" either to "Médecins Sans Frontières" or to any other translation of this name (including "Doctors Without Borders"). For example, in Iraqi Kurdistan, when presented with the acronym, respondents were convinced that the organization was part of the multinational armed forces lead by the United States. In Niger, some respondents in the villages around the City of Zinder thought that the red man on the MSF logo had his ribs out and, subsequently, they assumed that MSF was taking care of malnutrition in their country.

The research also identifies perception gaps related to the place of MSF as an institution that employs over twenty-seven thousand people and that has a budget of us$1 billion. It seems that MSF has trouble going from an associative management role to a more political role as a medical actor in complex emergency and political contexts. The example of Haiti shows that the role that MSF intends to play is not always the one that external actors or patients attribute to it.

In some of the countries visited for the study, strict MSF adherence to its independence principle led to its isolation from other actors in the field. For instance, in interviews with ICRC representatives, it was mentioned that it is important to be independent but that this should not prevent MSF from participating in coordination mechanisms, at least as an observer. The 2007 decision taken by MSF to refrain from participating in the UN cluster meetings in order to preserve its independence was not well understood by other actors because, in most cases, this decision and the logic behind it was not well explained.

The complex nature of the organization's structure and the existence of numerous MSF sections (e.g., MSF-Spain, MSF-Switzerland, etc.) appeared to create misconceptions among interviewees regarding the notion "without borders." Also, the way the organization manages the security of its teams was raised several times: in some countries, MSF staff live in compounds with high walls and have trouble integrating with the local population. Sometimes staff members have very little contact with the local community since, for security reasons, they have to circulate only between house and hospital. A reality check proved that the theory of "taking time and having tea" with the representatives of populations was very difficult to implement on a daily basis.

The question of the interdependence between emergency projects and development was raised many times during the research interviews. MSF always positions itself as a humanitarian medical organization that responds to emergencies; at the same time, however, many projects are planned to last several years. This duality creates a paradox: the organization feels that it is necessary to be involved in some contexts for a long time despite its emergency nature. Concerning humanitarian principles, in the beginning of the research it was presumed that everyone knew about MSF's

financial independence. In fact, only a few people reported knowing about the proportion of private donations in MSF's budget
(over 80 percent) or that there are some projects in which MSF does
not accept funding from governments (e.g., in Iraq and the occupied Palestinian territories). Moreover, each respondent gave a different definition of the humanitarian principles. This phenomenon
presents the organization with the challenge of translating its principles within the operational framework of its projects in the field.

Regarding one of the main aspects of the organization – "témoignage," or witnessing – most actors saw MSF as speaking out less
than other organizations (e.g., the ICRC), because of security
imperatives, need to have access to the population, and need to
witness/speak out in certain contexts (e.g., Sri Lanka, Yemen, and
the occupied Palestinian territories).

Also, MSF is using a military (and missionary) vocabulary
without being conscious of the impact this can have. There are
many terms that MSF staff use daily that some people consider to
be aggressive (e.g., "operational section," "plan of action," "headquarters," "compound," "head of mission," etc.). Given that MSF
claims to be a secular and independent organization, the use of
these types of terms creates a certain amount of confusion among
people in the field.

Perception of Humanitarian Action

Within the framework of this study, respondents were asked
questions related to their perception of humanitarian action in
general. Researchers expected certain answers (e.g., references to
the distance created by humanitarian assistance between the
North and the South, to NGOs sometimes being seen as a part of
the Western political agenda and representing Western interests,
etc.). The blurring of lines between the political agendas of some
actors, on the one hand, and the providers of independent humanitarian action, on the other, becomes even more complicated
when government representatives make unfortunate comments.
For example, French foreign minister Bernard Kouchner referred
to French humanitarian organizations as a "source of information"
during his October 2008 visit to the Gaza Strip.

Quite unexpectedly, in Cameroon, because of the presence of several Chinese actors, many thought that MSF was of Chinese origin. The comparison between MSF and Chinese actors was made according to such criteria as openness in managing security of staff, proximity to the local population, and the oriental medical approach of using herbs for treatment (an approach that was more understandable to people in Cameroon). This contrasted sharply with Western organizations and their apparent "paternalistic approach."

The issue of religion was mentioned many times in almost all contexts during the perception research. In Niger, for example, some respondents drew a link between the organization and charity, which, in turn, led to a sequence of assumptions that ended in the idea that MSF was an organization of Islamic origin and therefore based in the Gulf. This was neither confusing nor problematic for any of the respondents, but it illustrates the logic of people who are trying to understand MSF. Interestingly, in Guatemala it was clear that MSF did not have any links to religion and that, because of its Western origins, it was a very technical organization.

There is a gap between how MSF perceives itself and how others perceive it. The researchers examined perceptions related to MSF's identity, and it appears that various MSF sections have different understanding of MSF's institutional image, of témoignage, and of medical activities. The intention of this field research is to measure perceptions in a given context at a given time. Perception, of course, may evolve with a changing environment. Today, within MSF, perception analysis is becoming an integral part of the project analysis of host countries. It also influences how MSF trains newly recruited staff as well as middle and senior management (e.g., head of desk, head of mission, etc.).

A SPECIFIC EXAMPLE:
THE PERCEPTION STUDY IN CHAD

The following section presents some of the trends highlighted in the perception study conducted in Eastern Chad. MSF's long-term presence in this country, the characteristics of the humanitarian space on the border with Sudan, and the complex security issues were among the reasons we selected this particular context for a perception study. As the research further reveals, many perception issues identified in this context were also identified in other projects/countries and indicate the existence of very specific and systemic challenges for MSF in general rather than the isolated problems of a specific project.

Mission Context

MSF had been present in Chad since the mid-1980s.[3] In the eastern region, MSF-Switzerland (MSF-CH) could operate only after the end of hostilities in 2006, and it did so by opening projects in Guéréda and Adré (on the border with the Darfur region of Sudan).[4]

In 2008, MSF-CH launched a project on obstetrical fistula in Abéché Hospital,[5] Eastern Chad. The project had two objectives: (1) to contribute to the reduction of cases of obstetrical fistula in Eastern Chad and (2) to reduce the foetal-maternal mortality rate in the regional hospital of Abéché. Taking into account that fistula has both health-related and social side effects, the project was designed along three main axes:

- organizing and providing surgical services for women free of charge and improving health services for affected women in Eastern Chad;
- ameliorating services in the maternity ward of the regional hospital of Abéché; and
- sensitizing local population to fistula disease (main reasons and consequences).

MSF proposed creating a centre of excellence on fistula and contributing to the training of a national staff that would specialize in fistula. Patient services provided by MSF included all stages: screening, reception of patients, informing them about the disease and its treatment, confirmation of the diagnosis, surgery, post-surgical care, psychological support, and, when necessary, physiotherapy. In addition to medical activities, the project foresaw year-long communication activities in Abéché and the region in order to inform the population about the disease, the project, and

MSF services. The project was to be implemented in collaboration with the Ministry of Health, the local administrative authorities, and traditional leaders.

"Women's village" (VDF-village des femmes) was inaugurated on 1 October 2010 in Abéché. Initially, the project had to be implemented within a five-year time frame (2008 to 2012). Approximately sixty local staff members and seven expatriates were involved in implementing the project in October 2010.

Research Methodology

Information was collected during semi-structured interviews, individually or in groups, as per the approved questionnaire. This list of questions was used as a training tool for students from the Adam Barka University of Abéché to enable them to understand the scope of topics, the various aspects of perception, and the issue of translation.[6] Trained students collected information from urban and rural population as well as from women under treatment in VDF. Interviews with MSF interlocutors, stakeholders, and staff were conducted. The total number of interviewees exceeded five hundred persons (urban and rural populations). In addition, fourteen representatives of national and international NGOS, local authorities, media, and law enforcement bodies were interviewed in Abéché.

Does MSF Stand Out?

This study tried to define whether MSF was perceived differently from other actors; whether patients saw the difference between MSF and other humanitarian or national organizations; whether the outside perspective can make a clear difference between the humanitarians and the military; and so on. Answers to these questions varied according to the group category (authorities, local NGO, media, etc.), the type of interaction with the humanitarian organizations (beneficiaries, patients, partners, stakeholders, etc.), level of education, age, and sex.

It appeared that MSF was not sufficiently known to the general population (either urban or rural). There was also a great degree of confusion within the local population regarding what an NGO was and how different it was from the UN.[7] Reportedly, major parts of the population referred to all international organizations as NGOs and, in the case of MSF, referred to "one MSF" without differentiating according to operational sections. They remembered the name in French (Médecins Sans Frontières) but not its Arabic translation.

Many respondents associated humanitarian presence with aid to refugees but not with aid to the local population. A minority stated that some NGOs work with women and children. Respondents were not aware of the reasons for an NGO presence in Chad or why foreigners provided assistance to the local population. Many could not explain the difference between various organizations, and all foreigners were thought to belong to humanitarian organizations (ICRC, MSF, UN, and MINURCAT, etc.). It was confirmed that certain groups of the population (i.e., educated people, national staff of NGOs, local authorities, and military commanders) were better informed about the presence of MSF in general but not about the details of its action. Despite a generally hostile attitude towards foreigners in that area, MSF as a medical organization seemed to be in a more favourable position due to its presence in the Abéché hospital. All respondents said that MSF had a good image and was accepted by the local population. Three main factors were cited for the positive perception of MSF: (1) the medical action, (2) the quality of the provided service (e.g., a balanced approach between refugees and women from the local area), and (3) the adherence to MSF's institutional principles (impartiality, neutrality, and independence).

Concerning the appreciation of humanitarian aid (and the presence of foreigners in Abéché), the majority of respondents were not able to judge the efficiency of NGO projects, to respond to the presence of NGOs, or to know the difference between various actors. Most of the interviewees agreed that humanitarian assistance provided by foreigners (i.e., white people) was beneficial for the local population (despite an alleged negative impact on the local economy, internal politics, and increased population, etc.). Abéché residents reported that the security situation in their neighbourhoods had improved due to the presence of international

NGOS: security patrols circulated in the quarter, streets were lighted, and so on.

One particular finding was of special interest to the institution and was subject to an internal discussion. There were thirty-four women in the women's village who benefited directly from the MSF intervention. These women participated in the dissemination sessions organized by the MSF communication team and in the opening ceremony of the women's village. With regard to the question "Do you know MSF?" all respondents answered negatively. Nor, for example, were they able to identify the MSF logo. On the other hand, all interviewed women said that they were satisfied with "MSF assistance" (i.e., food, medical care, reimbursement of transportation fees, and supply of hygienic items). It seemed that these women did not see MSF as a separate entity, being convinced that it was a part of the Abéché Hospital facilities/project. In internal discussions, opinions were divided regarding whether MSF should be distinguished from local facilities (i.e., according to its impartiality, neutrality, and independence) or whether it would be better to blend with the local hospital structure (i.e., integration).

This study shows that MSF stands out as the only medical humanitarian organization. Its services, programs, and quality of treatment, along with its balanced approach (equal support to local/native population and refugees/IDP), were appreciated by the patients, stakeholders, and other NGOS. It appears that the MSF logo (not unlike any other logo) did not mean much to the recipients of aid or to the general population. Almost all respondents stressed the quality of action and its institutional principles as the criteria that distinguished MSF from other actors.

Communication Does Matter

An important part of the internal discussion based on the findings of this study was dedicated to the quality and objectives of MSF communication strategy. It was recognized that perception matters not only as a communication issue but also with regard to institutional positioning in the local context. Questions were asked about the quality of the dialogue with the local communities, with patients, between MSF and other actors as well as about methods of communication, their efficiency, and so on.

The study identifies the alleged "isolation" of MSF as one of the communication issues. The fact is that, because of security restrictions, MSF expatriates were able to move only in a limited space – from residence to the office or hospital. All external contacts were limited to a strict minimum and were in line with professional needs within the framework of the implemented project. There was no direct contact with the population, and the national staff was the only segment of the local population that interacted directly with expatriates. This resulted in limited knowledge of the social structure of the population, the inter-ethnic dynamic, and relations/contacts with the villages. Even in the town, expatriates were not always able to go to the local markets and have direct contact with the urban population in tea-houses or on the streets (in contrast to other contexts). These restrictions challenged the capacity of MSF to communicate effectively with the local community and other NGOs in Abéché. There was a need to find alternative solutions and innovative methods to enable MSF to inform the general population about the fistula project.

As an alternative solution, it was proposed to increase the number of information sessions on fistula and the fistula project. It was suggested that we start approaching village chiefs, men, and heads of households in order to inform them about the project and the disease and in order to obtain their permission to start an awareness-raising campaign for women. This had to be followed by a separate campaign dedicated to and targeted at women. It seemed that there was a need not only to inform about the disease but also to overcome certain stereotypes. Reportedly, women were not able to sell their craft pieces if it became known that they had fistula (as in the case of HIV, people did not want to touch these object for fear they would transmit a disease).

Another identified issue was linked to the fact that MSF was little known in the areas that were not affected by the Darfur crises. Respondents suggested reinforcing MSF's visibility through a number of actions: talks/tea conversations with the leaders in villages and in communities; dissemination sessions for the local authorities; and greater and regular accessibility to local media (as was often mentioned: "you come to radio only when *you* need *us*"). It was recommended that MSF hold regular meetings with media representatives to update them on MSF activities and to discuss areas of possible partnership with the local radio stations. Authorities and other NGOS suggested reinforcing MSF's communication with other actors and keeping them updated on MSF projects and activities. Many stressed the importance of sharing information on MSF principles, reasons for interventions, the history of MSF presence, and the objectives of institutional strategies at the local level, and so on.

Coordination and Collaboration

A need for meaningful collaboration between various actors (especially those working on fistula projects) used to be the subject of many conversations, even though it was not a part of the questionnaire developed for the perception study. A number of national and international interviewees stressed the high quality of the collaboration between MSF and hospital authorities. MSF medical expertise and professionalism were highly valued. At the same time, it was emphasized that, as a foreign medical NGO, MSF was perceived as being in competition with local doctors and traditional medical practitioners.

On coordination between various actors present in the hospital, interviewees expressed their wish for more meaningful actions in terms of harmonization of projects, payment methods, and approaches. Several collaboration initiatives were proposed that, it was thought, would be of benefit to the international NGO as well as to the hospital facilities (e.g., training of medical personnel, building of an incinerator, rehabilitation of canals and water supply systems in the hospital, etc).

Other actors (e.g., UNFPA) involved in the fistula-related activities in Chad expressed the desire to improve communication and collaboration between their project and that of MSF for reasons of efficiency, the planning of exit strategies, the better allocation of resources, and to ensure the coherence of messages.

The study findings emphasize the fact that people are willing to see MSF reinforce its collaboration and its systemic capacity to engage in a meaningful collaboration with other actors. They are also willing to see it coordinate its activities not only at the project level but also at the national and international levels with regard to policies aimed at enhancing the capacity of a country to respond to its local medical needs. Feedback from the study respondents suggests that, within the existing operational space, MSF, as a leading humanitarian actor, needs to pay more attention to the quality of communication, information sharing, and analyses of its impact than do other NGOs.

PERCEPTIONS OF MSF'S INFLUENCE ON SECURITY

Understanding the influence of various perceptions of MSF actions and principles on the security of humanitarian workers was one of the key aims of this perception study.[8] Historically, many humanitarian projects in Eastern Chad were initiated in relation to the Darfur crisis and the massive influx of a displaced population.[9] Abéché was a convenient logistical base at which to run operations in IDP camps, but the local population did not benefit from humanitarian assistance. There were allegations that the economic conditions in Abéché had worsened since the arrival of foreigners. The Abéché population increased due to the presence of military forces and, as many Chadians came to Abéché seeking employment, prices on major products increased and, due to increased demand, water became even scarcer. After the mass arrival of international NGOs and other actors (2003–04), which led to a dramatic change of the demographic, political, and economic face of Abéché, many NGOs reduced their projects and, by 2008–09, some had entirely withdrawn from the region. This created another wave of hardship due to decreased employment opportunities, with the price of major necessities remaining high.

Many within MSF and many of those interviewed had a strong impression that the Zoe's Ark scandal (2007) seriously compromised humanitarian space and trust in humanitarian actors.[10] MSF personnel felt that the controversial history of humanitarian presence, along with the numerous national as well as foreign military personnel present in Abéché, influenced the perception of the local population. Among that population, many seemingly did not see any difference between the UN peacekeeping mission (MINURCAT),[11] other military and/or law-enforcement bodies, and humanitarian NGOs. Due to a number of security incidents, some foreign NGOs accepted armed escorts, and this fact complicated local perceptions even more.[12]

The gap in communication between the local population and foreigners was also increased by the restrictions that were imposed for reasons of security. Typical comments were: "They only have visual contacts with foreigners passing by in cars; they don't know much about each other and don't understand each other; it creates not only concerns but also suspicion and aggressive attitudes towards foreigners." In addition, people felt that many NGOS arrived with predefined and well-funded projects that often did not take into consideration the needs of the local/native population. For example, Abéché was used as a coordination or logistical base for humanitarian projects implemented outside the Abéché area.

MSF seemed to be one of the rare organizations that strictly followed its guiding principles of impartiality, neutrality, and independence. MSF's rejection of military armed escorts did not please military authorities, but it was respected and admired by other international organizations. At the same time, many interviewees felt that rigorous observation of institutional independence led to the team's being isolated and detached from the current reality in the town. It was recommended that MSF inform the population about its principles, especially since some national associations and NGOS claimed to operate on the basis of those same principles. Many mentioned issues of cultural awareness and local traditions as potential sources of security incidents.

Measuring the Impact of MSF

The question of MSF's impact on the health situation was asked in order to measure the efficiency of the institutional medical interventions and to identify potential for further developments.

Collected information indicated that MSF's influence went beyond its medical action.

First, MSF was named as an important economic actor and as a good employer. For example, the hospital nurses employed by MSF for VDF program were satisfied with the salary level offered by MSF. Because of MSF's experience and in-house training with regard to fistula, these nurses hoped to be knowledgeable enough about the disease to find employment after MSF's eventual departure.

Second, many respondents expressed their concern about the lack of coherence in exit strategies and in how MSF closed its medical projects. They gave some examples of when MSF's abrupt departure from projects resulted in difficulties for local populations. Reportedly, these included the inability of local authorities to respond appropriately to local needs: not only did patients lose access to the medical supply, the quality of care go down, and the number of doctors/medical personnel decrease dramatically, but the population also had to pay for all services and drugs.

MSF actions seemed to have tremendous influence on the motivation of national staff members and their engagement with humanitarian organizations. National colleagues who had worked for several years with MSF explained that, at first, they were simply looking for employment but then became committed to a humanitarian cause. Even though MSF's salary was much lower than those of other organizations, many said that they preferred to stay with MSF and to make their career within it. Participation in internal debates was seen as a sign of prestige and recognition. Many national employees in Abéché stressed the value of MSF program-related training and/or its contribution to the general education of its staff.

MSF's presence in Abéché (like that of any other NGO) resulted in an unprecedented influx of Chadian workers from other provinces and, with this, tensions between national staff and residents of Abéché regarding regional and economic issues. Allegations of protectionism and cultural insensitivity led to increased suspicion of expatriates and relocated national staff. Revised MSF human resources policies and recruitment practices seemed to have resulted in improved communication and the balanced geographical representation of key national staff.

MSF seemed to underestimate its impact on Abéché Hospital's working culture. The perception study suggests that MSF should analyze and more efficiently manage the changes in local structures and environment triggered by its projects and interventions. Hospital authorities appreciated MSF's contributions to its maternity ward, which included improvements in sanitary standards, discipline, quality of medical care, outcomes, and so on. However, they also mentioned that there was little or no coordination between MSF and the hospital with regard to supervision of local staff, changed job descriptions, and daily training of national personnel. The study suggests that MSF should not replace hospital rules but, rather, coordinate its activities with those put in place by local authorities.

CONCLUSION

Although, so far from answering all questions, this MSF perception study reveals new issues (many of which had already been second guessed by the institution), it nevertheless provides a wider perspective on the way MSF operates. While it confirms that MSF stands out as a medical humanitarian organization, the perception gaps it identifies only reinforce existing institutional challenges. It also confirms that perceptions vary greatly between population groups. Not surprisingly, the study finds that diverse perspectives and definitions are influenced by many factors: local culture, history of relations between actors, politics, individual interests, and distribution of power.

NOTES

1 Caroline Abu-Sada, ed. *In the Eyes of Others: How People in Crises Perceive Humanitarian Aid* (New-York: MSF/Humanitarian Outcomes/ NYU Center on International Cooperation, 2012).

2 See Antonio Donini, *The State of the Humanitarian Enterprise.*
   Medford: Feinstein International Center, 2008.

3 For more information, see *Chad: Powder Keg in the East,* Crisis Group
   Africa Report 149, 15 April 2009; *Chad: Escaping from the Oil Trap,*
   Crisis Group Africa briefing 65, 26 August 2009; *Tchad: Au delà de
   l'apaisement,* Crisis Group Africa Report 162, 17 août 2010.

4 See http://www.msf.ch/nos-projets/ou-nous-travaillons/en-bref/tchad/
   (viewed March 2012).

5 Approximately 2 million women in Africa have a fistula, which is a
   hole between the vagina and the bladder or rectum through which
   urine or faeces leak continuously. Fistulas can be caused by prolonged
   obstructed labour and childbirth or by sexual violence in addition to
   lack of medical facilities. Women with fistulas are often outcasts from
   their communities because of the smell associated with the leaking of
   urine/faeces, and, in some cases, they are abandoned by their husbands.
   Chances for women to have their fistula repaired are slim as many hospitals and health clinics do not have the proper instruments or knowledge and skills to carry out such a procedure. See: http://msf.org/msf/
   articles/2011/03/fistula-reconstructive-surgery-returns-lives-dignity-
   and-well-being.cfm (viewed March 2012).

6 MSF recruited students or external researchers from local universities
   in all contexts in which the perception study was conducted. This was
   done primarily because of language barriers (knowledge of local
   dialects was required) and in order to collect more accurate and
   independent data from the local population.

7 For more details, see Abu-Sada, *In the Eyes of Others.*

8 Helle Garro, "Does Humanitarian Space Exist in Chad?"
   Humanitarian Exchange Magazine, December 2008, 39–41. See also
   Lauren Ploch, "Instability and Humanitarian Conditions in Chad,"
   Congressional Research Service, July 2010. Available at http://www.
   fas.org/sgp/crs/row/RS22798.pdf.

9 Clea Kahn and Elena Lucchi, "Are Humanitarians Fueling Conflicts?
   Evidence from Eastern Chad and Darfur," *Humanitarian Exchange
   Magazine,* June 2009, 20–3.

10 In late 2007, Chadian authorities nabbed a group of European aid
   workers for attempting to evacuate 103 children to France.

11 Diana Felix da Costa and John Karlsrud, "A Role for Civil Affairs in Community Conflict Resolution? MINURCAT's Intercommunity Dialogue Strategy in Eastern Chad," *Humanitarian Exchange Magazine*, October 2010, available at http://www.odihpn.org/humanitarian-exchange-magazine/issue-48/a-role-for-civil-affairs-in-community-conflict-resolution-minurcats-intercommunity-dialogue-strategy-in-eastern-chad.

12 François Grunewald and Olivia Collins, *The Three Pillars of Humanitarian Space in Chad*, September 2010, available at http://www.urd.org (viewed December 2011).

2

At the Limits of Perception:
Humanitarian Principles in Action[1]

FRANÇOIS COOREN AND FRÉDÉRIK MATTE

The desire to be viewed in a favourable light implies the desire for recognition – recognition of what singles us out, what differentiates us, and what drives us as individuals or as an organization. Thus, we seek to project traits that are meant to characterize us and to shape our identity. This projection comes through the values and principles for which we profess attachment and that are supposed to constitute not only our being but also our rationale for our actions. In other words, we seek to influence the views of others through what we do and what we claim to represent. While such a proactive approach is, in part, within our own competence, it is nevertheless, as Erving Goffman clearly shows,[2] dependent upon the persons on whom we are attempting to make a "good impression." Interpreting how others say they perceive us has its limits since this "management of impressions" is engaged in by all concerned and at every moment. It is therefore difficult to know what others really think, believe, or perceive about what we are or claim to be because the reflections that they hope to return to us also include their share of projection and performance.

Our study, "At the Limits of Perception," seeks to analyze how MSF's actors engage in their daily humanitarian work, particularly when they interact with their partners or communicate with patients or representatives of the populations affected by their actions. This analysis, which involves five years of observation in MSF missions around the world, enables us to study how, on a daily basis, this humanitarian organization's representatives attempt to manage the perceptions they wish to create and to control. Complementing the "perception" studies carried out by MSF Switzerland, this communication-oriented ethnographic approach allows us to take a look at personnel and what might be called their "routine work of projection" – a work that takes place, as we attempt to show, one interaction at a time and that is reiterated and replicated.

After providing the general context of our research program, we explain that it is based on what we call a "constitutive" vision of communication.[3] By this we mean that communication constitutes and shapes the mode of being and operation of any organization and/or collective.[4] Studying the ways in which an organization's members communicate means studying the various ways in which an organization operates, or functions, on a daily basis. As we attempt to show, this mode of operation proceeds through the principles, values, and standards of action that MSF's actors embody, implicitly or explicitly, in their daily interactions and activities. To speak metaphorically, we might say that these actors "ventriloquize" these principles/values/standards. In other words, they make them speak, thereby legitimizing their position and attempting to manage impressions by putting on a good face.

However, beyond the effects of ventriloquism, it is the tensions among the figures that embody these principles/values/standards in which we are particularly interested. Working in difficult situations, as MSF's personnel very often do, means being faced with situations in which principles or standards of action are in apparent tension with one another. This obliges these personnel to make decisions and/or to find compromises. Thus, in investigating all the figures that MSF's actors make use of in their daily activities, we also witness the tensions they experience. This illustrates the complexity of MSF's work and identifies lessons that could prove valuable in terms of training and preparation for future missions.

OUR RESEARCH PROGRAM:
CONTEXT AND METHODOLOGY

We have now been working with MSF for more than five years. This collaboration was initiated with the French branch of the organization from 2005 to 2008 and, since 2009, has been pursued with MSF Switzerland. The general objective of our research is to better understand and analyze what MSF's actors and representatives do on a daily basis, aside from conducting interviews and other formal discussions, which are always subject to the distortions of a posteriori reconstruction. Thus, with a camera, we followed MSF's actors in order to record their daily activities as faithfully as possible. Whether they were regional coordinators, heads of mission, field coordinators, logistics officers, administrators, nurses, or doctors, all strove to act and communicate on behalf of the organization – and this is the activity that, in all its complexity and contingency, we attempted to capture.

Over the years, our methodology, which is known as "videoshadowing," enabled us to gather several hundred hours of video recordings from all over the world, whether at headquarters in Geneva or Paris, at the logistics centre in Bordeaux, or (especially) in one of the ten missions that MSF coordinates and to which we had access – Kenya (Dadaab Camp), Mozambique (Maputo), Swaziland, Democratic Republic of Congo (North Kivu and Kampala), Jordan (Amman), Djibouti, Sri Lanka (Jaffna Peninsula), and Niger (Zinder). The data collection method was always the same: our video camera followed one or more MSF actors as they conducted their routine activities, which included meeting with political and army officials, directors of hospitals, and other NGOs as well as internal discussions involving only MSF personnel.

Out of all the data gathered, we were mainly interested in what seemed to motivate the various positions/decisions taken by MSF representatives. In other words, we wanted to better understand the principles, values, and standards that not only embodied the daily work of MSF but that also made a difference to it. We wanted to grasp these principles/values/standards in action.[5] Once this data had been selected, we retranscribed it and then organized dozens of data analysis sessions, during which we patiently worked to reconstruct the driving forces of humanitarian action. In the following section, we briefly explain our method of analysis, which is based on a particular conception of communication.

COMMUNICATION AS VENTRILOQUISM

The communication perspective that we adopt begins from the observation that any action raises the question of its legitimacy,[6] or at least of its rationale.[7] Officially, MSF presents itself as motivated by a mandate that "consists in providing emergency medical assistance."[8] It might therefore be said that any action or decision taken by the representatives of this humanitarian organization should, in theory, be driven by the mandate that its founders provided at its creation in 1971. This mandate (among others) is what legitimates MSF's ability to state that it is within its rights when it provides aid, and acts as it does, in a given region of the world.

What we propose, metaphorically, to call ventriloquism involves acting or speaking for something or someone.[9] This term, which is borrowed from the world of theatre, signifies that acting or speaking always presupposes *causing* someone to act or *causing* someone to speak. This idea may be found in such expressions as "What makes you say/think that?" or "What led you to do that?" These are questions that call upon us to justify and explain our positions or actions. What particularly interests us in the activity of ventriloquism is the ambiguity with which it surrounds the origin of action. To be sure, the ventriloquist animates the dummy, which is also referred to as a *figure*, but it could just as easily be said that the dummy animates the ventriloquist. Since the figure has to be animated, *the ventriloquist is made to speak by what he or she ventriloquizes.*[10]

This same oscillation, which is identified by D. Goldblatt,[11] is found in *any* form of communication. Thus, for MSF to intervene in the name of its mandate, either explicitly or implicitly, is not only to legitimize its action but also to indicate that it is authorized by mandate. To give expression to or to carry out a mandate – that is, to embody it in a discussion or a mission – also implies that this mandate animates us and that we are, to a certain extent, subjected to it. Indeed, MSF points this out on its website, which states: "All MSF workers agree to subscribe to the principles set out in the Charter."

To conceive of communication metaphorically as an act of ventriloquism is, as we stated above, to uphold a constitutive vision of it.[12] Anyone who has worked in an organization knows that it is through interactions that decisions are taken and communicated, that it is through interactions that one acts on behalf of an organization, and that it is through interactions that one debates the principles, values, and standards that should govern interventions. By advancing the idea of ventriloquism, we simply want to highlight the fact that, in all these interactions, many things, or figures, are communicated and made to speak: not only passions, interests, attachments, concerns, and emotions but also cynicism, despair, and resentments.

In the course of our research we sought to identify in our recordings all the figures that MSF's representatives strove to cultivate through their exchanges. We accordingly identified what these figures expressed and, at the same time, what caused them to speak or act, thereby justifying, authorizing, or explaining their positions, decisions, and actions. Beyond the organization's official positions, we wanted to decipher what seemed to drive MSF's humanitarian action on a daily basis, knowing that its Charter no doubt played a large role in this but that other figures may also have come into play.

In connection with the concept of perception, we show that to be perceived in a certain way is to be seen as embodying or representing certain figures (values, principles, identities, emotions, sentiments, etc.). These are the figures to which we are attached and/or that dwell within us. To express resentment or cynicism, for example, is to show that one is in the grip of (or even beset by) this particular type of feeling. To defend a principle is to show that one is attached to it and claims to act on its behalf. In the two cases in question (attachment and in-dwelling), it is understood that, if one gives expression to these figures (i.e., if one makes them say something), it is because they themselves are also supposed to make us speak. Perception therefore implies a constant play of representation in which, although one indeed tries to make a *good* impression, one may also, depending on the circumstances, make a mediocre or even a poor impression.

Above and beyond perception there is interaction, transaction, exchange, and communication – all those activities by which multiple figures are expressed and cultivated and that we have to identify and analyze, thereby opening a window onto what might be called the "MSF culture" (since culture is indeed all that is cultivated). In particular, we were interested in the *tensions* that MSF's actors might experience daily. These tensions might take the form of the coexistence of several figures deemed incompatible, opposed, or contradictory.

In a fairly recent work, speaking of organizations in general, Cooren, Taylor, and Van Every say: "Members are ... balanced between independence and cooperation, centralization and decentralization, flexibility and coordination. Organizational communication implies navigating between unity and diversity, between integration and differentiation."[13] MSF, like any organization, experiences tensions, but we have to identify which ones by means of our theoretical and methodological approach. Accordingly, we define tensions as situations in which certain figures contradict others by the fact that they appear to dictate at least two types of behaviour that are deemed to be opposing, contradictory, or incompatible.

Thus, going back to the preceding quotation, it might be noted that any organization is, in principle, beset, inhabited, or haunted both by a desire for independence and by a desire for cooperation (a situation that any MSF representative surely knows very well). These two principles may be in tension to the extent that a desire for independence might dictate an action (e.g., the taking of a unilateral decision to cancel a mission) that is incompatible with a desire for cooperation.

Feeling a tension (either because one experiences it as an intervener or perceives it as an observer) therefore means finding oneself in a situation in which figures dictate at least two lines of conduct that deemed to be incompatible with one another. In the name of the principle of independence, we do not have to justify or account for our decision to cancel a mission, while in the name of the principle of cooperation, we may well have to negotiate the conditions of cancellation or even question its pertinence.

In our analyses we have therefore attempted to identify not only the figures that were cultivated in the discourse and conduct of MSF representatives but also (and especially) the tensions that attachment to these figures generated. In particular, we studied how MSF's interveners routinely managed and negotiated these tensions, which, in our view, is an integral part of their work.

SOME KEY FIGURES AND TENSIONS

Let us begin with some key figures that, according to our observations, are very often invoked by MSF's actors. In what follows, we explain how they are given expression and, especially, what purpose they serve in action and interaction. We then take up the issue of the tensions to which these figures give rise.

Seven Key MSF Figures

To identify these figures we viewed several hours of video recordings in order to isolate those particular figures that seemed to be constantly invoked in discussions. Recordings from MSF actors and third-party MSF agents (such as representatives of NGO partners, local medical staff, or soldiers) were examined. We identified seven figures that, in our view, constitute part of MSF's daily reality. These figures, in no particular order, are: Geneva, experience, security, independence, proximity, the patient, and quality of care.

GENEVA
No one who has worked for MSF will be surprised that the image of the headquarters is ventriloquized by aid workers in the field. We might even go so far as to say that some heads of mission seem literally haunted by this authority figure, asking themselves

out loud, for example, what Geneva would think of such and such a situation. Much reference is therefore made to Geneva, which is invoked to justify or postpone a decision or to complain about a lack of understanding on the part of headquarters.

Thus, accordingly, we often observed heads of mission legitimizing their decisions by stating: "Geneva wants that." This enabled them to blame the unpopularity of a decision on headquarters. Even if the mission was thousands of kilometres from the Swiss city, it was felt to be very *present* in the discourse and action of interveners, indicating the mission's attachment (in both senses of the term "attachment" – constraint and interest) to the words, attitudes, and directives of headquarters. To refer to Geneva in a given discussion is, therefore, to attribute to that city actions, decisions, feelings, or positions that are weighty enough to make the difference in determining what position will be taken.

For example, some actors may cite the figure of Geneva to justify a decision that is overdue because it is still awaiting the approval of managers at headquarters. One of the field coordinators put it this way: "It can just take a bit of a process to turn away, for Geneva to make their decision. At the end of that, it's their decision." In other words, the decision-making process, while inclusive in some regards, finally rests with "Geneva" and the de facto authority conferred upon it. Thus, the evocation of, and justification associated with, the term "Geneva" allows the person citing it to avoid taking personal responsibility for a decision applied in the field.

Another illustration involving a field coordinator (FieldCo) and a logistics coordinator (LogCo) further demonstrates how the term "Geneva" can be mobilized and ventriloquized in the field. This is an excerpt from a conversation regarding the future orientation of their mission in Somalia.

LogCo: But still, we don't have a clear strategy and a clear overview of what's going to happen. Maybe soon but …
FieldCo: Yeah, well, obviously we're going to have a lot of opinions on the situation but hopefully Geneva can understand and …

LogCo: But I mean, we cannot go on like this for a long time.

FieldCo: No, no, no.

LogCo: We really have to take a deci... or Geneva has to take a decision.

FieldCo: But it really has to come from here into the field with the support of Geneva.

LogCo: Yes of course.

We see here how the FieldCo immediately adopts the stance of waiting on Geneva, hoping that it (in the end, the "it" that Geneva really represents does not matter) will eventually understand the situation and formulate a clear strategy for the mission. Then – and this is where it becomes fascinating – the LogCo begins his reply by saying, "We really have to take a deci..." only to correct himself in the middle of the word "decision" and refer to Geneva as the entity that will finally make the determination. Afterwards, we see a kind of shift take place. The LogCo at first takes a stance involving "we," meaning Geneva and the field, and then proceeds to make a distinction between these two entities, demonstrating the ambiguity that can exist between them. However, we see that the FieldCo responds by reducing the ambiguity: the decision will have to be taken in the field and then be supported by Geneva. He cites the figure of Geneva in his response but puts the field first. From this excerpt, it can be seen that the field and headquarters engage in a sparring match to determine who has power and authority. Clearly, Geneva is a figure that is omnipresent (and possibly omnipotent) to the eyes of the field coordinators.

EXPERIENCE

Although less explicitly expressed than the figure of "Geneva," the figure of experience has a great deal of weight and importance in the discourse and action of MSF. It frequently occurs in conversations among MSF members and often seems to be invoked to win influence, credibility, and even authority. In a sense, to take a stance as a full-fledged MSF worker means to make use of this basic figure/value as often as possible. This is because it permits

MSF members, from the first mission staff member to the old humanitarian crusader, to mutually evaluate each other.

But making use of the figure of experience is also a way of justifying an action or a decision. To make experience speak is to ventriloquize a certain reality and to add its weight to one option over another. In discussions of ideas, we found that many narratives were used to establish one's credibility and the strength of certain positions. Consider, for example, the following heated discussion between a regional coordinator (RC) and a FieldCo, which took place after a stormy meeting with a hospital director who was annoyed by MSF's repeated interventions (the purpose of which was to change the establishment's procedures):

RC: That – oh, at first, it was hard in Baruba too, it was not all that easy, but after, uh, two, three, four months, it started to get easier because in the end reality catches up with all of us [laughs].

FieldCo: Yeah, but you see, there are some situations, I don't want it to catch up with us, yeah. In some situations, I don't want a decision to be taken after there is a kid who croaks.

RC: No, no, no, I mean reality in the sense of the concrete, by doing things that –

FieldCo: Yeah, yeah.

RC: In time, they come to realize themselves that we make them change lots of things, we reorganize lots of things. It's confrontational for them, eh? That's normal, you can't [shakes his head "no"], you can't always show them how to do something saying, "everything is bad, your way, you have to change everything," because they get fed up.

FieldCo: Well, no, no. At the same time, you don't do it like that, you see ...

RC: No, you don't do it like that, that's why it takes time, that's why it takes more than, that it takes discussions and sometimes it's exasperating and [laughs], but, well [shakes his head], it's the same everywhere.

FieldCo: Yeah, yeah, well ...

RC: It's still better here because, in Sudan, damn it, the discussions [shakes his head still more] you can't even imagine [continues to shake his head].

FieldCo: Oh, I was in Nigeria, it was the same there.

RC: Oh there, it's ...

FieldCo: It was much the same in Nigeria [muffled laughter].

RC: Hours and hours and hours of discussions that never lead anywhere.

While the regional coordinator cites his experience in Sudan to show his interlocutor that patience in this type of situation always pays off (reality always catches up to us, in his view), the field coordinator replies by citing his experience in Nigeria. This leads him to cite some of his unfortunate experiences in that region. Thus, he implies that patience leads nowhere and that, at some point, if you do not want the lives of patients put in danger, you have to impose certain procedures. This shows how experience may make the difference with regard to justifying, or dictating, one mode of conduct rather than another.

SECURITY

In principle, security is an issue that should never be called into question. As soon as the issue of a mission's security is invoked during a discussion it can supplant all other issues, including what is supposed to be MSF's raison d'être – the care of patients. However, in practice, when it is deemed that the risks incurred are manageable, security is a figure that is simply one among others.

We note, however, that the figure of security is very useful for justifying decisions. Moreover, it is often presented as non-negotiable, which means that, once invoked by a head of mission or desk officer, it may quickly inspire a whole series of actions, ranging from the cancellation of an intervention to the complete withdrawal of the mission itself. For example, a head of mission based in Nairobi, Kenya, had to take the decision to withdraw a person from a mission for constantly questioning the security regulations. It should be said that the location in question, the refugee camp of Dadaab (at the Somali border), was deemed very "risky" for the staff. Indeed, MSF had received threats that its employees would be kidnapped in order to secure a ransom. In fact, security regulations were a key issue in Dadaab and a great source of concern, both at headquarters in Geneva and on site. This particular person, however, seemed to find the regulations in place too strict and therefore questioned the authority of the field coordinator, frequently denigrating his capacity to take enlightened decisions. Regardless of whether or not this account is true (we had only the head of mission's version), the fact is that the person questioned the sacrosanct principle of security, thereby tarnishing the authority of the coordinator. The head of mission justified his decision as follows: "We cannot have somebody on the ground that is constantly questioning and reanalyzing security ... because it's one thing when you have small discussion within the team because of small incidents. But it's quite something else when you have a critical incident."

In a situation in which security might have been less of a concern, such questioning would probably have been tolerated or even encouraged. However, in this context, the head of mission decided that security was more vital than allowing a challenge to authority and MSF regulations. This decision was all the more difficult because the person in question, who was later dismissed from the mission, was recognized as being competent in his area of expertise. It may therefore be assumed that the issue of security prevailed over the issue of criticism. Although MSF prides itself on being an organization in which one can easily criticize managerial decisions, one cannot trifle with security. At least, this was the interpretation adopted by the head of mission at the time.

INDEPENDENCE

Independence is a very prominent figure in MSF's approach to its mission and is very likely the one that most differentiates MSF from other humanitarian organizations. There is a feeling that independence is extremely relevant to MSF personnel, particularly in contexts in which the need for aid and resources is pressing and in which MSF has been actively sought out. MSF's independence is a major concern of MSF's officials, all the more so because it is frequently called into question. Independence becomes particularly relevant when MSF is induced to make concessions in order to maintain its presence in a region and still manage to provide quality care to a population.

Moreover, the figure of independence is often used to differentiate MSF from other organizations, which, in many cases, are beholden to government financial supporters. When it comes to the question of security, we can almost speak of an MSF ethos. This ethos can sometimes seem like arrogance (particularly in the eyes of competing organizations) or even indifference. Nevertheless, it allows MSF to constantly reaffirm its own values, especially when it is a question of not losing sight of the plight of people and patients in danger. For this reason, the figure of independence is always carefully safeguarded.

In Maputo, the capital of Mozambique, we were able to see the extent to which MSF's independence was a constant concern for the officials of an HIV/AIDS mission. How did MSF assert its independence when it seemed to have lost some control over how HIV/AIDS patients were treated and given follow-ups? While MSF officials praised the desire of the local government to look after its own patients, they criticized the lack of human, logistical, and financial resources that prevented that government from effectively taking care of its own citizens. In the final analysis, MSF officials decided that they were making too many concessions and, thus, were sacrificing the issue of the independence of their medical approach to the issue of respect for the national sovereignty of the host country.

PROXIMITY

As with independence, the figure of proximity seems to be a constant MSF concern, particularly with regard to patients. First and foremost, MSF defines itself as an organization comprised of doctors and nurses, which means that, in the final analysis, its most important actions are medical. However, to act or to speak in the name of this figure is also to take very concrete decisions that, for example, lead to MSF's setting up close to refugee camps or in regions where many organizations no longer dare to go.

Proximity is therefore a figure that inspires MSF's daily actions and discourse. It is necessary to be on site and to go to see what is happening, but it is also necessary to show the population that you are close to them. To set up in or around a refugee camp is therefore not only to get close to populations in danger but also to try to communicate to them that MSF values proximity, despite the security risks it entails.

It is this kind of concern that prompts MSF representatives to walk every morning and every evening to the shantytown of Kibera in Nairobi, Kenya, when security concerns would dictate that they take a car. It is this same kind of concern for proximity that motivates MSF when it decides to set up on the border of the camp in Dadaab, when all the other NGOs are located in a highly secure UN compound thirty minutes from the camp by car.

THE PATIENT AND QUALITY OF CARE

Other key figures of MSF's action and discourse are the patient and the quality of care provided, and these inspire many discussions, whether between partners or among MSF interveners themselves. Their centrality is evident from MSF's almost total lack of compromise. For instance, MSF's officials are prepared to pay more if the quality of medication warrants (indeed, quality is very precisely monitored by the organization).

We also noted that it is often in the name of quality of care and patient well-being that tensions arise between partners, particularly when it is a matter of questioning the routines of a hospital that is receiving operational and financial support from MSF. It is as though patients play the role of a catalyst in the organization's actions – a catalyst on whose behalf MSF may question often well-established local medical practices. From one point of view, it is this constant concern for the patient that results in MSF's being criticized for taking a position that some would call neo-colonialist. In the name of the patient's health, MSF may shake up medical and hospital practices by attempting to impose what it regards as the right approach to treatment.

TWO MAIN TENSIONS

As stated above, all the figures that we have listed correspond to what is conveyed, or ventriloquized, in the discourse and interactions of MSF's interveners. But, as we also noted, these figures are also what is supposed to inspire these same interveners whenever one of them follows a particular line of conduct. For example, to speak for a patient and his/her well-being is to imply that certain actions should be taken, which, in the opinion of the MSF intervener, effectively promote the patient's health. This same reasoning, of course, also applies to the other six figures identified. To position oneself implicitly or explicitly as a spokesperson for these figures is to claim that the action they authorize is beneficial.

The fact remains, of course, that different actions may be taken depending on the figures that have been invoked. It should also be noted that the same figure can often be ventriloquized in several ways (to mean several things), tracing lines of conduct that might be deemed incompatible. This is what we observed a number of times when we felt that MSF representatives were being torn between principles of action that seemed incompatible or contradictory, or again when we saw the same principle invoked by two respondents to justify two opposite types of interventions.

While many others could be identified, we deal here with just two tensions that seem to be characteristic of the action and discourse of MSF. These tensions are (1) distance versus proximity and (2) independence versus cooperation. In what follows, we have made a concerted attempt to explain the logic of these tensions, a logic that we illustrate with concrete examples drawn from our observations.

Distance versus Proximity   As we note above, proximity is one of the essential figures of MSF's approach. And this is not surprising, given the identity of the organization, which is centred on the patient and the medical act. However, the principle of proximity is often balanced by other lines of conduct that indicate the need for a certain distance either between MSF and the populations it serves or between the coordinators and the personnel in the field. Obviously, one of the reasons for this is security. Thus, we saw that MSF consciously decided to allow its personnel to walk through the shantytown of Kibera to reach the clinic. This decision was designed to indicate MSF's proximity to the local population. However, there is also a fair bit of distancing. This is symbolized by guards with walkie-talkies, who accompany the MSF medical personnel during their travels on foot, and by the T-shirts sporting the MSF logo worn by all MSF personnel.

Distance is also to be seen in the attitude of the coordinators when they spoke to us about their relations with the heads of mission in the field. One of them stated: "So you should be on the frontline and close. It's great and it's out with the people and proximity and blah, blah, blah ... But a lot of the job is coordination. And if you don't want to be a field coordinator and do the coordination ... Coordination means coordinating. So it doesn't mean being always out there."

For this coordinator and many others, the work consists in managing a certain distance (or, conversely, a certain proximity) in relation to the various sites of which he or she is in charge. Such decisions often bring tensions, which are very difficult to manage – as difficult as the tensions that characterizes the relations between MSF and the populations it is supposed to help.

Independence versus Cooperation This is no doubt the most common tension among MSF representatives, who are very attached to the independence of the MSF approach to medical care for endangered populations. As we previously noted, MSF intervenes in regions of the world where, very often, basic resources are cruelly lacking, with the result that the organization is often approached. Conversely, MSF knows very well that the effectiveness of its activities depends on the cooperation of government and local authorities (as in the case of Maputo) as well as on the cooperation of all kinds of intermediaries and interlocutors, from the advocacy worker who mobilizes targeted fringes of the population to the local doctors who must choose to transfer their patients from local health centres to MSF-supported hospitals.

In this context, the main fear is instrumentalization, which is experienced as the loss of the independence of action so dear to MSF. To instrumentalize the organization's activities is to risk deviating from what MSF sees as its principal line of conduct: caring for the fate of populations in danger (and, to an extent, criticizing the conditions in which these populations find themselves). MSF's response might be characterized as the management of controlled and limited cooperation, which amounts to managing the tension between a degree of interdependence and a degree of dependence within any given environment. To be sure, any cooperation requires that at least some of MSF's activities be instrumentalized, but it is out of the question that this instrumentalization should result in MSF's deviating from the course it has set for itself.

This tension is seen, for example, in a discussion between an MSF representative and two local officials of the Congolese department of health. The two government representatives appealed to MSF for assistance in training doctors in their region. The MSF representative replied by explaining that, although MSF was not a university, the local doctors might be able to develop their skills "on the job" by working with MSF's volunteer doctors. This indicates a desire to collaborate and, indeed, the acceptance of a kind of instrumentalization – but it is an instrumentalization limited by the desire for independence. MSF is first and foremost an organization centred on medical action: it is not a training centre, as such.

CONCLUSION

Clearly, perception, as we conceive it, is a matter of figures. To perceive someone or something is also to perceive that that person or organization represents or embodies principles, values, sentiments, realities, and so on. If we wish to be perceived as independent, as close to populations, or as experienced, then we need to embody independence, proximity, and experience. Therefore, it is necessary that these figures occur not just in our discourse but also in our practices and activities, whether walking in the shantytown of Kibera or setting up on the margins of the Dadaab camp.

Our message is that the perception of MSF is something that is constructed one interaction at a time. It is mediated through discourse and through a multitude of figures that are implicitly or explicitly ventriloquized. These figures often authorize, justify, or explain MSF's positions and decisions, but they also take form operationally – that is, in the field. To plead to see humanitarian principles in action is, above all, to plead that MSF's humanitarian interventions communicate the principles they are meant to embody.

NOTES

1 We wish to thank Chantal Benoit-Barné and Boris Brummans for the valuable assistance they provided in the writing of this document. Our sincere thanks also go to the MSF officers and volunteers who generously agreed to cooperate in this research.

2 E. Goffman, *La présentation de soi* (Paris: Éditions de Minuit, 1973).

3 F. Cooren and F. Matte, "For a Constitutive Pragmatics: Obama, Médecins Sans Frontières and the Measuring Stick," *Pragmatics and Society* 1, 1 (2010): 9–31.

4 L.L. Putnam and A.M. Nicotera, eds., *Building Theories of Organization: The Constitutive Role of Communication* (New York: Routledge, 2009).

5 F. Cooren, F. Matte, J.R. Taylor, and C. Vasquez, "A Humanitarian Organization in Action: Organizational Discourse as a Stable Mobile," *Discourse and Communication* 1, 2 (2007): 153–90.

6 C. Benoit-Barné and F. Cooren, "The Accomplishment of Authority through Presentification: How Authority is Distributed among and Negotiated by Organizational Members," *Management Communication Quarterly* 23, 1 (2009): 5–31.

7 F. Cooren, J.R. Taylor, and E.J. Van Every, eds., *Communication as Organizing: Practical Approaches to Research into the Dynamic of Text and Conversation* (Mahwah, NJ: Lawrence Erlbaum, 2006).

8 MSF website: www.msf.org.

9 F. Cooren, B.H.J. Brummans, and D. Charrieras, "The Coproduction of Organizational Presence: The Case of Médecins Sans Frontières in the Democratic Republic of Congo," *Human Relations* 61, 10 (2008): 1339–70; Cooren and Matte, "For a Constitutive Pragmatics," 9–31; F. Cooren, "Comment les textes écrivent l'organisation: Figures, ventriloquie et incarnation," *Études de communication* 34 (2010b): 23–40; F. Cooren, "Ventriloquie, performativité et communication: Ou comment fait-on parler les choses," *Réseaux* 28 (2010c): 35–54.

10 Cooren, "Comment les textes écrivent l'organisation," 23–40.

11 D. Goldblatt, *Art and Ventriloquism: Critical Voices in Art, Theory and Culture* (London/New York: Routledge, 2006).

12 K. Ashcraft, T. Kuhn, and F. Cooren, "Constitutional Amendments: 'Materializing' Organizational Communication," *Academy of Management Annals* 3 (2009): 1–64; Nicotera Putnam, "Building Theories of Organization: The Constitutive Role of Communication," *Administrative Science Quarterly* 55, 1 (2010): 159–61.

13 Cooren, Taylor, and Van Every, *Communication as Organizing*.

3

The Nigerian Lead-poisoning Epidemic: The Role of Neoliberal Globalization and Challenges for Humanitarian Ethics

JOHN D. PRINGLE AND DONALD C. COLE

INTRODUCTION

The lead-poisoning epidemic in northern Nigeria has been devastating. To date, more than four hundred children have died (over 40 percent of the children in one village alone), and there is an entire generation of village residents at risk of death or serious irreversible short- and long-term health effects.[1] First detected in March 2010, it has been described as unprecedented, the worst such outbreak in recorded history.[2] One report states: "Never before has there been a lead poisoning epidemic of this magnitude anywhere in the world."[3]

Shortly after the onset of the epidemic, I (first author) arrived as the epidemiologist with the MSF emergency response team. While others in the team set to work establishing emergency treatment centres, I worked within the communities to document and mitigate the disaster as well as to organize groups of children to come to hospital for chelation therapy. For two months on site, I witnessed the nature of their poverty and the disastrous consequences of unsafe artisanal mining. The situation made me reflect on my previous mission with MSF in northern Nigeria, which was in response to epidemics of meningitis. It led me to ask why there is such a need for so many projects run by international organizations. As my colleagues often asked, why is MSF so involved in northern Nigeria when Nigeria is one of the wealthier countries in sub-Saharan Africa and there is no war? This chapter uses a political economy approach to unveil the important social, political, and economic (i.e., the societal) forces that precipitated this epidemic. It argues that poverty, inequality, high gold prices, and lack of essential public health services created the context for the epidemic and that all of these phenomena have their roots in neoliberal globalization. The forces of neoliberal globalization are also felt within international humanitarianism, posing fundamental ethical challenges for international aid organizations.

OVERVIEW OF THE EPIDEMIC

In February 2010, a number of young children in Yargalma, a remote rural village in northern Nigeria, were acutely ill and dying. The local community health worker administered the last of his meagre drug supply with no effect. He reported the problem to his superior, but, rather than receiving immediate assistance, he received more antimalarial drugs of the kind that had proven useless (personal communication with health worker). Meanwhile, the children of Yargalma continued arriving at his clinic with lethargy, fever, vomiting, weight loss, bulging fontanels, nuchal rigidity, partial paralysis, and seizures. Many more would die. On 29 March 2010, an outbreak surveillance team from MSF heard about the deaths and, after witnessing the crisis first-hand, assembled a team to provide twenty-four-hour medical care for the children. Was this a new infectious disease? While signs and symptoms resembled meningitis and cerebral malaria, those treatments remained ineffective.

Mothers of the sick children disclosed to the health workers that there had been an increase in the number of rock-grinding machines and gold-extraction activities in the village around the time of the first deaths. The price of gold had been surging as a result of the recent global financial crisis. Men from several villages in northern Nigeria began processing locally mined ore to extract gold, and this resulted in an increase in artisanal mining. These were poor subsistence farmers, but, by extracting flecks of gold, they hoped to improve their meagre incomes.

With special government permission, MSF sent blood samples to an accredited lab in Germany for analysis and was notified of the results: the children had very high lead levels, ranging from 109–370 mcg/dl (personal field note from meeting with MSF coordinators). For children, a blood lead level of ten is considered elevated, and a level greater than one hundred is considered fatal.[4] These lab results led to a fuller investigation of artisanal mining in and around homes and villages as the source of heavy metal contamination. An ore of high lead content, some exceeding 10 percent lead by weight, had entered the chain of production.[5] While the village of Yargalma was at the epicentre of the epidemic, numerous other villages were also highly contaminated.

MSF responded to the outbreak by providing twenty-four-hour on-site medical care, establishing two field hospitals, providing free emergency chelation therapy for the worst affected, helping to organize remediation efforts, and advocating for improved health services for this vulnerable population.[6] By this point, aid workers understood how rural poverty, along with high gold prices, could create an increase in artisanal mining. However, without proper safety measures or public health capacity, the outcome was a humanitarian disaster.

CONTEXT OF POVERTY AND INEQUALITY

Nigeria is the most populous country in Africa, with over 150 million people and an approximately equal division between the mainly Muslim north and Christian south. Poverty is dire, and its effects are obvious: even before the lead-poisoning epidemic, Nigeria had some of the highest mortality rates in the world for infants and child-bearing women.[7]

The World Bank classifies Nigeria as a lower-middle-income country, so one might expect to find poverty and an underfunded health system.[8] However, Nigeria has experienced an average annual growth in real GDP of 7 percent (2003–08).[9] Nigeria is a member of the Organization of Petroleum Exporting Countries (OPEC), and its oil exports are at an all-time high.[10] Nigeria is the largest oil producer in Africa and the eleventh largest producer of crude oil in the world. The petroleum industry constitutes approximately 80 percent of national revenues.[11] Much of this inflow is deposited in the federal Excess Crude Account. Also known as the National Sovereign Wealth Fund, this government account was established in 2004 to de-link public expenditures from oil revenue volatility. Oil revenues above a set benchmark price are deposited into the account, with the objective of protecting planned budgets against shortfalls due to volatile oil prices and improving macroeconomic stability.[12]

Towards the end of 2008, about $30 billion sat in Nigeria's Excess Crude Account. By early 2011, the fund had trickled down to about $300 million, with $15 billion spent in 2010 alone.[13] As financial analysts and government-watch groups argue: "When oil prices are high, money flows into the account, and it becomes an irresistible, unaccounted-for jackpot, especially for the largely autonomous governors of Nigeria's 36 states."[14]

In the context of such wealth's availability to national and state governments, its allocation elsewhere reflects different priorities and political will rather than a question of adequate finances.[15] Decision makers are actively underfunding both the determinants of health (education, housing, and livelihoods) and the health system to such an extent that an average of approximately 2,300 under-five-year-olds and 145 women of childbearing age die each day, making Nigeria the second largest contributor to the under-five and maternal mortality rate in the world.[16] As an example of other national expenditures, Nigeria participates in UN peacekeeping missions. Currently, Nigeria is one of the largest troop-contributing nations in the UN, with close to five thousand troops deployed around the world as of 30 April 2011 representing close to 6 percent of troops in the UN Peacekeeping Operations.[17]

· Poverty is worse in northern Nigeria than in the rest of the country and highest for those living rurally. Poverty is socially constructed, as noted by the prominent anthropologist Marshall

Sahlins: "Poverty is not a certain small amount of goods, nor is it just a relation between means and ends; above all it is a relation between people. Poverty is a social status. As such it is the invention of civilisation. It has grown with civilisation, at once as an invidious distinction between classes and more importantly as a tributary relation."[18]

All northern states have poverty levels greater than 60 percent, with averages of 80 percent in the northwest and northeast.[19] And, while poverty declined in most of Nigeria between 1996 and 2004, it increased in parts of the north.[20] Maternal and child health, while among the worst in the world in Nigeria, is critically dire in northern Nigeria.[21] In northwest Nigeria, 43 percent of the children under the age of five are underweight, compared to 17 to 19 percent in the south.[22] Polio and measles have significantly diminished in the south but persist with high morbidity and mortality in the north, posing a threat to neighbouring countries.[23] Such excruciating poverty leads to high numbers of children and adults flocking from villages to cities in search of a better life and to the ubiquitous *Almajirai*, or street children, begging for survival.[24]

While the northern economy is dependent on agriculture, it is also necessary to improve many other sectors in order to address the chronic state of poverty and inequality. As the governor of Niger State succinctly remarked: "Agriculture is a veritable vehicle for the development of northern Nigeria while development goes beyond purchase of tractors and fertiliser as there is more to the politics and economics of it."[25]

UNDERSTANDING THE ROOT CAUSES
OF THE EPIDEMIC

Artisanal mining is a mining activity in which a person labours at extracting certain minerals by rudimentary means and with a minimal amount of capital or equipment. This mining activity is often informal and illegal. Globally, an estimated 13 to 20 million men, women, and children from over fifty developing countries are directly engaged in the artisanal mining sector, and an estimated 100 million more are indirectly dependent on the sector for their livelihood.[26]

A joint CDC/WHO/MSF investigation team determined the cause of the epidemic based on on-site epidemiological, clinical, and laboratory research. In their report, the cause of the epidemic is described as follows:

> The increased mortality was the result of acute lead poisoning, determined to be caused by massive environmental contamination from artisanal mining and processing of gold found in lead-rich ore. The grinding of the ore into fine particles resulted in extensive dispersal of lead dust in the villages concerned, including within family compounds. Ingestion and inhalation of the fine lead particles was determined to be the major reason for high blood lead levels in victims' bodies.[27]

Given this explanation, it is clear that the CDC/WHO/MSF team understood the cause of the epidemic from a *biomedical model* perspective, as evidenced by its mechanistic explanation of how the lead makes its way into victims' bodies. This provides an important link in the causal pathway, but it does not explain the whole story: Why was there a lead poisoning epidemic? Why these people, in this place, at this time?

A field worker with TerraGraphics, the agency tasked with environmental remediation, provides a further explanation as to the cause of the epidemic:

> Women and children usually stay inside the compounds all the time, which exacerbated the impact of the contamination. I'd go inside the home with a female translator and map the compound, asking questions about where they worked with the ore. We measured the soil and dust in the home with an x-ray fluorescence (XRF) device and usually found it to be highly contaminated with lead. We observed them prepare meals and noticed how they laid out their food on the contaminated ground to dry and then pulverized it in the same

mortar and pestle that had been used to grind the ore. We saw children playing in contaminated soil. Basically, they were engulfed in contamination.[28]

This explanation describes behaviours that exacerbated the uptake of lead into bodies. It is an explanation founded on the *behavioural model*, in that it presents the lead poisoning is a consequence of household actions and individual behaviours. Again, this is an important link in the causal pathway but does not fully address our questions.

Some media reports go further and describe the contextual factors surrounding the epidemic. Once example is from the Associated Press:

The existence of gold deposits in this area along the border of Niger had been long known. But it wasn't until gold prices soared in recent years that villagers began heading into the bush to search for it. Soon the poor herdsmen and farmers could sell gold for more than $23 a gram – a huge sum in a country where most people live on less than $2 a day.[29]

From such accounts, we learn that affected families may have engaged in artisanal mining out of desperation, tempted by an extremely high commodity price to improve their situation by mining for gold. This last explanation takes a political economy approach, emphasizing the economic context of the epidemic. In order to fully understand the aetiology of the epidemic and why there was a need for an international response, it is necessary to consider societal forces.

POLITICAL ECONOMY

The *political economy* approach to epidemiology attempts to understand the broader political and economic structures that influence health and disease distribution.[30] It focuses on how the market and economics, political ideology, and other forces are integrally related and affect public health policy.[31] Looking beyond the social determinants of health to include the broader political and economic (i.e., the *societal*) determinants of health,[32] political economy examines interactions among the local, regional, and global levels, including the historical context from which the determinants evolved.[33] It further explores the interactions of race and class as they affect the allocation of power and privilege.[34] It considers the vulnerability, or powerlessness, of a population,[35] analyzed as a political and economic process. The political economy approach takes into account the proximate biomedical and behavioural aspects but adds the broader political, economic, and social context.[36] Hence, in this chapter, we use a political economy approach to examine the societal forces, or the societal determinants of health, that affected the Nigerian lead-poisoning epidemic.

From a *micro*economic viewpoint, although an increase in household income would reduce the allure of gold extraction, the dangerous activity will continue so long as poverty persists. Health education, lead exposure prevention, and harm-reduction initiatives (all of which MSF and other organizations have undertaken in affected villages) are important public health interventions. However, high gold prices will outweigh marginal improvements in risk awareness. An unintended consequence of free chelation treatment and environmental remediation may be a lowering of the expected cost of artisanal mining and, indeed, may inadvertently promote its continuation. Given a risk-benefit analysis, the key forces in the epidemic are: (1) baseline income and (2) gold prices.

For the lead poisoned villages of northern Nigeria, income from subsistence farming, in the face of low prices for produce and increasing prices for inputs, is synonymous with poverty. Given the paucity of social welfare provision, the costs of life's necessities further reduce meagre incomes. People pay out of pocket for essential services such as health care and education, despite (and often due to) their poverty.[37] Hence they are primed to take on artisanal mining and processing activities.

The *macro*economic system behind the poverty and high gold prices is the *cause* of the cause of the epidemic.[38] This system includes social, political, economic, and historical contexts; social policies and government regulations; and living conditions. Within all levels of the macroeconomic system lie inequality and the forces of economic globalization.

GLOBALIZATION AND NEOLIBERALISM

According to Joseph Stiglitz, the Nobel laureate in economics, globalization is "neither good nor bad";[39] rather, it is "the closer integration of the countries and peoples of the world which has been brought about by the enormous reduction of costs of transportation and communication, and the breaking down of artificial barriers to the flows of goods, services, capital, knowledge, and (to a lesser extent) people across borders."[40] Stiglitz argues that, in its current form, globalization is not working for many of the world's poor: poverty is soaring, household incomes are plummeting, and disparities in wealth are growing. However, the problem is not with globalization per se but, rather, with international financial institutions. These institutions, both private financial corporations and more public institutions such as the International Monetary Fund (IMF), the World Bank (WB), and the World Trade Organization (WTO), systematically favour the interests of the more advanced industrialized countries over those of the developing world.[41]

To understand the influence of international financial institutions, it is necessary to understand the neoliberalism that drives their policies:

> Neoliberalism is a theory of political economic practices that proposes that human well-being can best be advanced by liberating individual entrepreneurial freedoms and skills within an institutional framework characterized by strong private property rights, free markets and free trade. The role of the state is to create and preserve ... those military, defence, police, and legal structures and functions required to secure private property rights and to guarantee, by force if need be, the proper functioning of markets. Furthermore, if markets

do not exist (in areas such as land, water, education, health care, social security, or environmental pollution) then they must be created, by state action if necessary.[42]

The main tenets of neoliberalism are: the rule of the market; the cutting of public expenditure for social services; deregulation; privatization; and the elimination of the concept of "the Public Good" in favour of the notion of the free functioning of global, national, and regional markets. Neoliberalism has its roots in the capitalist crisis of the early 1970s.[43] During that time, the US Federal Reserve chairman Paul Volcker sharply increased interest rates. This "Volcker shock" made Nigeria's debt soar from $9 billion to $29 billion.[44] After decades of development, modernism, and enticements to borrow heavily, poor countries suddenly found themselves with huge and unmanageable debts.[45] Bankers and corporate lenders continued to receive their debt payments, while social programs and essential public services were gutted.[46]

Neoliberal globalization runs contrary to global public health. The loss of health care protections and the increasing imposition of multiple-layer user fees add to the financial burdens of the poor and the sick.[47] The role of the IMF and neoliberal ideology in undermining global efforts to combat HIV/AIDS is well documented.[48] With the lead-poisoning epidemic, the affected population in northern Nigerian was and remains at risk.

The lead-poisoning epidemic occurred in a time of global financial crisis. Through a complicated global economic network, investors rapidly invested in gold, thereby creating demand and raising gold prices globally: "Western investors' new interest in gold has coincided with the rich world's deepest period of economic turmoil since the 1930s ... As long as the world economy remains uncertain and investors fear inflation and sovereign default, gold will keep its allure."[49] The fact that the demand for gold in London and Delhi was felt in northern Nigeria is a testament and defining feature of globalization, an increasingly powerful societal determinant of health.[50]

The financial crisis created economic shockwaves around the world, pushing national governments to prioritize economic recovery over public health programs.[51] International financial institutions shared the same priorities: "The mantra of the World Bank initiatives, 'improve the economy and everything else will follow,' included health, not as a right, but a 'responsibility' that those benefiting from a strong economy would buy."[52] Yet this period saw an overall net reduction in expenditures for public health, health care, education, and development. In this context, MSF was left to respond to the Nigerian lead-poisoning crisis.

INTERNATIONAL HUMANITARIAN SECTOR

Humanitarianism, a term "fraught with ambiguities," can be defined broadly as an ideology, a movement, and a profession.[53] Among those in the international humanitarian sector, humanitarian aid involves the provision of emergency medical and essential public health services to save lives, to alleviate suffering, and to maintain and to protect human dignity during and in the aftermath of large-scale emergencies. Generally thought to be a short-term intervention distinct from longer-term development aid (though the reality is often otherwise), it strives to observe the humanitarian principles of impartiality, neutrality, and independence.[54] For the purposes of this chapter, humanitarianism is what Donini refers to as the *humanitarian internationale*,[55] represented by the familiar Northern/Western humanitarian NGOs with expansion into the Global South. The point here is that, regardless of the definitions one adopts and of the personal motivations of those involved, humanitarianism in its Northern and Western incarnations is increasingly consubstantial with processes of economic, social, and cultural globalization and, more often than not, with world ordering and securitization agendas.[56]

Globalization played a large role in the Nigerian lead-poisoning epidemic; it also played a large role in the international humanitarian response. As efficient as global economic markets may be, they fail to address fundamental human needs such as adequate and safe food, shelter, water, and livelihoods. While the World Bank's (publicly stated) mission is to eradicate poverty, the humanitarian response to public health emergencies is relegated to international humanitarian organizations.[57] Particularly since the 1980s, NGOs have expanded and multiplied under neoliberalism.[58] As a consequence, international humanitarian action can undermine a government's responsibility to provide essential services. NGOs are stepping into the vacuum left by the withdrawal of state governments from social service provision (some refer to this as privatization by NGOs).[59] Humanitarian action under current forms of globalization raises serious ethical issues, as the Nigerian lead-poisoning epidemic demonstrates.

Given the absence of an adequate disease-outbreak surveillance system, the lead poisonings in northern Nigeria quickly escalated into a large epidemic. The disease-outbreak surveillance system in northern Nigeria has long been known to be inadequate. In prior years, meningitis epidemics have flourished in remote rural areas before health officials became aware of them.[60] In 2006, I (first author) was project coordinator and epidemiologist on an MSF project that conducted its own meningitis surveillance. Our strategy was active case-finding, exploring remote rural villages for evidence of cases that exceeded the epidemic threshold.[61] The rationale for such a project was that, by identifying meningitis outbreaks early, we could launch a timely vaccination program and prevent further spread. We were well aware that early detection was unlikely under the current national surveillance system.

During the start of the lead-poisoning epidemic in March 2010, an MSF team was (yet again) actively searching for clusters of meningitis cases. Its inquiries brought it to the epicentre of the lead-poisoning epidemic in Yargalma and the emergency response began. Soon other international organizations were invited to respond, including the US Centers for Disease Control and Prevention (CDC), the Blacksmith Institute, and TerraGraphics.[62]

While the CDC conducted rapid household surveys and Terra-Graphics prepared for environmental remediation, it was MSF that provided the emergency medical response. MSF delivered immediate medical support on site as soon as the epidemic was confirmed and then quickly established field hospitals to treat those worst affected. All in-patient children were provided with free chelation therapy, comorbidity treatment, and meals for themselves and their adult caregiver (usually the mother).[63] From the beginning, MSF stressed to its partners that its intervention was an emergency humanitarian intervention, not a comprehensive one. Yet, as we approach the end of 2011, there are still many people with dangerously high blood lead levels (e.g., older children) in need of medical attention. Perhaps more troubling are the numbers of previously treated children who are returning with elevated blood lead levels (personal communication from field staff).

HUMANITARIAN ETHICS

Humanitarian ethical issues deserve attention because international humanitarian aid organizations are subject to the same globalization forces that are implicated in the lead-poisoning epidemic. And, when it comes to these forces, humanitarian aid organizations are not neutral. By responding to emergencies such as the lead-poisoning epidemic, international organizations create a parallel health care system that may compete with the national system or partially absolve the national and regional governments of their responsibilities.

Other ethical issues also arise. In responding to an emergency, international organizations may usurp local material supply chains and draw on meagre human resources. Pulling local health professionals from local ministries of health is a recurrent issue as international NGOs tend to offer better wages and working conditions. While the urgent need to save lives and alleviate suffering can justify emergency interventions, there may be an increasing dependence on international aid organizations to fill the health system void created by chronic neglect.

An international medical humanitarian aid organization such as MSF does not confine itself to emergencies in war zones: it also provides services in situations in which local health systems are overwhelmed or decayed. The health contexts are often quite similar, with outbreaks of preventable diseases (such as cholera and measles) compounded by acute and chronic malnutrition, and inundated by the unmet needs of mental illnesses, obstetrical emergencies, and violence-related injuries. And, while civilians in war qualify for protection under international humanitarian law, there is no equivalent law for civilians subjected to neoliberal policies.

The humanitarian sector may be growing in relation to need, but, at the same time, it may contribute to a positive feedback loop: as the humanitarian sector grows, government investment in essential public services may decline further. International humanitarian organizations like MSF strive to observe the humanitarian principles of neutrality, impartiality, and independence. In the case of the lead-poisoning epidemic, the principles of neutrality and independence are at stake. Neutrality is an issue as MSF may be perceived to be siding with neocolonial capitalist forces by assisting the mining sector (i.e., by fixing its occupational health problems). Independence is an issue as MSF may be perceived to be a puppet of the political and economic status quo (i.e., by filling in for the Ministry of Health). MSF's medical care provides a stark illustration: it is precisely because health, and therefore medical care, is so vital to every individual that the provision of medical care often comes to represent the benevolent face of an otherwise unequal and divided society. People who are sick are extremely vulnerable, and the ultimate demonstration of concern on the part of the state is to care for its citizens when they are ill (or even to save them from death).[64]

In a medical emergency, recipients are concerned about getting care, not about who is providing that care. And, by responding to such disasters as the lead-poisoning epidemic, MSF may unwittingly endorse neoliberal economic austerity by cushioning its effects.[65] As one researcher states: "Humanitarian assistance remains a fig leaf covering the absence of political action."[66]

While the actions of the MSF field workers saved many lives, questions remain regarding the longer-term duty to care. In my (first author) personal interactions, I shared concerns with health workers about discharging severely and permanently lead-damaged children back to their villages, in which there are no apparent resources to properly care for them. Was it simply our job to save their lives? Can we justify our short-term commitment by arguing that we are only an emergency response organization? Do we satisfy our ethical obligations by transferring our patients' care to an ill-equipped or absent local Ministry of Health? Issues regarding duty to care certainly are not new to humanitarian aid work, and this angst is at the heart of témoignage.

TÉMOIGNAGE

So what of témoignage? This term, frequently used by MSF, denotes the act of humanitarian workers' speaking out about what they have seen in their line of work. It denotes a willingness to speak out in the interests of populations in danger and to bring abuses and intolerable situations to the public eye. It is a component of advocacy, a rallying cry for an end to the extreme suffering experienced by civilians and witnessed in solidarity by humanitarian aid workers.[67]

Given the dire and ongoing situation of the Nigerian lead-poisoning disaster, engaging in témoignage may help to improve the long-term outlook for those affected. It may also help international humanitarian aid organizations shed their neocolonial image and advocate for improvements in disease surveillance and essential public health services. This may be done in conjunction with other groups involved in counter-movements,[68] exposing neoliberal globalization as detrimental to global public health security. Humanitarian aid workers, their beneficiaries, and their strategic partners will have to decide if and how témoignage may be of benefit.

CONCLUSION

The Nigerian lead-poisoning epidemic is an example of dispossession on the part of neoliberal globalization. While the lead-rich ore was the product of nature, the neoliberal context was not. By applying a political economy analysis, this chapter demonstrates that the Nigerian lead-poisoning epidemic occurred within a context of poverty, inequality, high gold prices, and a lack of essential public health services. High gold prices were a result of the recent global financial crises. This created an opportunity for poor local villagers and subsistence farmers to supplement meagre incomes. However, without adequate safety measures or essential public health services, their efforts resulted in tragedy. This tragedy necessitated an international response. And while governments and global financial institutions abandon the needs of the poor, international humanitarian aid organizations like MSF increasingly fill the void.

MSF provided an emergency humanitarian response, saving lives and alleviating suffering. However, MSF's intervention comes with important ethical implications. For example, free chelation treatment and environmental remediation may lower the expected cost of artisanal mining, thus inadvertently ensuring that it continues. Creating a parallel health care system appropriates local materials and human resources from struggling local government agencies and opens the door to privatization. By providing band-aid solutions to the consequences of neoliberal globalization and public health neglect, MSF may be perceived to be contravening the humanitarian principles of neutrality and independence. Témoignage is an avenue through which to address these issues and to advocate for marginalized and dispossessed populations. By identifying the societal causes of humanitarian disasters, public health advocates and humanitarian aid workers will be better informed and equipped to oppose neoliberal forces in the interest of global public health security.

NOTES

1 Blacksmith Institute, UNICEF program cooperation agreement, *Environmental Remediation: Lead Poisoning in Zamfara, Final Report* (New York, NY: Blacksmith Institute, September 2010–March 2011), available at http://www.blacksmithinstitute.org (viewed 22 December

2011); CNN, "Aid Groups Say Lead Poisoning Has Killed 400 Children in Nigeria," available at www.CNN.com (viewed 6 October 2010).

2 CNN, *Gold Rush Triggers Deadly Lead Poisoning in Nigeria*, available at www.cnn.com (viewed 30 November 2010); C.A. Dooyema et al., "Unprecedented Outbreak of Acute Childhood Lead Poisoning – Zamfara State, Nigeria 2010," *Environmental Health Perspectives* 120, 4 (2012): 601–7; L. Shanks, "Responding to Lead Poisoning in Nigeria," paper presented at MSF, Conference Plenary Presentation, Canadian Conference on Global Health, Ottawa, Canada, 2010.

3 Blacksmith Institute, *Environmental Remediation*, 22.

4 Committee on Environmental Health, "Lead Exposure in Children: Prevention, Detection, and Management," *Pediatrics* 116, 5 (2005): 1036–46.

5 Blacksmith Institute, *Environmental Remediation*.

6 Shanks, *Responding to Lead Poisoning*.

7 Agence France-Presse, UN *Chief Visits Nigeria in Wake of Landmark Vote*, available at http://www.google.com/hostednews/afp/article/ALeqM5jXgemqxLMGti7hmEqFJeezT6hiUA?docId=CNG. b4eb7b7b77167ad494e2239eff1c3199.12b1 (viewed 22 May 2011); UNICEF Nigeria, *The Children: Maternal and Child Health*, available at http://www.unicef.org/nigeria/children_1926.html (viewed 29 May 2011).

8 World Bank, *Country and Lending Groups: Data*, available at http://data.worldbank.org/about/country-classifications/country-and-lending-groups (viewed 5 May 2011).

9 The Economist, *Pocket World in Figures: 2011 Edition* (London: Profile Books Ltd., 2010).

10 "Nigerian Oil Exports to Hit Six-Month High in June," *Reuters*, 28 April 2011.

11 W. Wallis, "Excess Crude Account: Rainy Day Fund Runs Dry," *Financial Times*, 29 September 2010, available at http://www.ft.com/reports/nigeria (viewed 22 December 2011).

12 SWF Institute, "Sovereign Wealth Fund Institute: Nigeria," 2008, available at http://www.swfinstitute.org/fund/nigeria.php (viewed 28 May 2011); S. Usman, *Nigeria: Scorching the Natural Resource Curse*, paper presented by the Honourable Minister of Finance, Federal Republic of Nigeria, London, United Kingdom, 26 January 2007.

13 A. Nossiter, "Riches Flow into Nigeria, But Are Lost after Arrival," *New York Times*, 8 February 2011.

14 Ibid.

15 R. Patel, *The Value of Nothing: Why Everything Costs So Much More Than We Think* (Toronto: HarperCollins, 2009), 118. He challenges the conventional notion of "a lack of political will," arguing that it misrepresents the nature of the problem. While the will of the public is to defend the public good (e.g., accessible health care, education, clean water and sanitation, protecting the environment), the will of government representatives is often to serve corporate and self-interests. Therefore, political will is subverted rather than lacking.

16 UNICEF Nigeria, *The Children*.

17 United Nations, "United Nations Peacekeeping: Troop and Police Contributors," available at http://www.un.org/en/peacekeeping/resources/statistics/contributors.shtml (viewed 21 May 2011).

18 M.D. Sahlins, *Stone Age Economics* (Chicago: Aldine-Atherton, 1972), 37.

19 For these statistics, material poverty is defined as an income of less than one dollar (N$129) per day, or less than N$3,870 per month. The legislated national minimum wage is N$5,500 per month. Therefore, based on the 2006 Census, more than 52 million people in the north live below the poverty line. See A.Y. Bello, *A Case of Irresponsible People in Government? What Soludo's Revelations Translate to for North – Economist (interview with Malam Salihu Lukman)*, message posted 26 July 2008 at http://nigeriavillagesquare.com/forum/main-square/21688-poverty-northern-nigeria-full-disclosure.html; H.J. Ibrahim, *Poverty in Northern Nigeria: Full Disclosure*, available at http://nigeriavillagesquare.com/forum/main-square/21688-poverty-northern-nigeria-full-disclosure.html (viewed 20 May 2011).

20 UNDP, *Human Development Report Nigeria, 2008–2009: Achieving Growth with Equity* (Abuja, Nigeria: United Nations Development Programme, 2009).

21 H.V. Doctor, R. Bairagi, S.E. Findley, S. Helleringer, and T. Dahir. "Northern Nigeria Maternal, Newborn and Child Health Programme: Selected Analyses from Population-Based Baseline Survey," *Open Demography Journal* 4 (2011): 11–21.

22 UNDP, *Human Development Report Nigeria.*

23 IFRC, *Annual Report: Global Measles and Polio Initiative 2008* (Geneva: International Federation of Red Cross and Red Crescent Societies, 2009).

24 M.T. Aluaigba, "Circumventing or Superimposing Poverty on the African Child? The Almajiri Syndrome in Northern Nigeria," *Childhood in Africa* 1, 1 (2009): 19–24.

25 H.J. Ibrahim, "Nigeria: North's Vicious Circle of Poverty, 26 July 2008, available at http://allafrica.com/stories/200807280573.html (viewed 29 May 2011).

26 S. Darby and K. Lempa, "Advancing the EITI (Extractive Industries Transparency Initiative) in the Mining Sector: Implementation Issues," produced with support of EITI Multi-Donor Trust Fund, 2007, pp. 1–15.

27 UN Office for the Coordination of Humanitarian Affairs (OCHA) and UNEP, *Lead Pollution and Poisoning Crisis, Environmental Emergency Response Mission, Zamfara State, Nigeria* (Geneva: Switzerland: Joint UNEP/OCHA Environment Unit, 2010), 5.

28 TerraGraphics, "Zamfara State Leads Cleanup Project, Nigeria," 2010, available at http://www.terragraphics.com/Projects/Nigeria.aspx (viewed 28 April 2011).

29 J. Gambrell, "Lead Poisoning Outbreak Causes Emergency in Nigeria," Associated Press, 7 January 2011.

30 L. Doyal and I. Pennell, *The Political Economy of Health* (London: Pluto Press, 1979); N. Krieger, "Proximal, Distal, and the Politics of Causation: What's Level Got to Do with It?" *American Journal of Public Health* 98, 2 (2008): 221–30.

31 D. Raphael, "Social Determinants of Health: Present Status, Unanswered Questions, and Future Directions," *International Journal of Health Services* 36, 4 (2006): 651–77.

32 I. Kawachi, B.P Kennedy, and R.G. Wilkinson, *The Society and Population Health Reader: Income Inequality and Health* (New York: The New Press, 1999), 1:xix–xxiv; D. Raphael, "A Society in Decline: The Social, Economic, and Political Determinants of Health Inequalities in the USA," in *Health and Social Justice: A Reader on Politics, Ideology, and Inequity in the Distribution of Disease*, ed. R. Hofrichter, (San Francisco: Jossey-Bass, 2003).

33 V. Navarro, ed., *The Political Economy of Social Inequalities: Consequences for Health and Quality of Life* (Amityville, NY: Baywood, 2002).

34 M. Minkler, "The Political Economy of Health: A Useful Theoretical Tool for Health Education Practice," *International Quarterly of Community Health Education* 15, 2 (1994): 111–26; Navarro, *Political Economy of Social Inequalities*.

35 S. Collinson, "Humanitarian Action in Conflict: Implementing a Political Economy Approach," *Humanitarian Policy Group Briefing* 8 (2003): 1–4.

36 A. Birn, Y. Pillay, and T. Holtz, *Textbook of International Health: Global Health in a Dynamic World*, 3rd ed. (New York: Oxford University Press, 2009), 132–40.

37 L.A. Amaghionyeodiwe, "Government Health Care Spending and the Poor: Evidence from Nigeria," *International Journal of Social Economics* 36, 3 (2009): 220–36.

38 A. Birn, "Making It Politic(Al): Closing the Gap in a Generation: Health Equity through Action on the Social Determinants of Health," *Social Medicine* 4, 3 (2009), 166–82, esp. 172.

39 J.E. Stiglitz, *Globalization and Its Discontents* (New York: W.W. Norton, 2003), 20.

40 Ibid., 9.

41 Ibid.

42 D. Harvey, *A Brief History of Neoliberalism* (Oxford: Oxford University Press 2005), 2.

43 E. Martinez and A. García, *Neoliberal Defined*, 2000, available at http://www.globalexchange.org/campaigns/econ101/neoliberalDefined.html (viewed 10 January 2011); Harvey, *Brief History*.

44 N. Klein, *The Shock Doctrine: The Rise of Disaster Capitalism* (Toronto: A.A. Knopf, 2007).

45 Harvey, *Brief History*.

46 W. Ellwood, *The No-Nonsense Guide to Globalization* (London: Verso, 2001).

47 Harvey, *Brief History*.

48 R. Rowden, *The Deadly Ideas of Neoliberalism: How the IMF Has Undermined Public Health and the Fight Against AIDS* (New York: Zed Books, 2009).

49 "Gold: Store of Value," *Economist Magazine*, 8 July 2010, available at http://www.economist.com/node/16536800.

50 R. Labonté and T. Schrecker, "Globalization and Social Determinants of Health: The Role of the Global Marketplace" (part 2 of 3), *Globalization and Health* 3, 6 (2007): available at http://www. globalizationandhealth.com/content/3/1/6.

51 R. Beaglehole and R. Bonita, "Public Health and Neo-Liberalism: Response to a Commentary," *European Journal of Public Health* 8, 4 (1998): 331–3; Klein, *Shock Doctrine*.

52 F.M. Burkle, "Future Humanitarian Crises: Challenges for Practice, Policy, and Public Health," *Prehospital and Disaster Medicine* 25, 3 (2010): 195.

53 A. Donini, "The Far Side: The Meta Functions of Humanitarianism in a Globalised World," *Disasters* 34 suppl. 2, 2 (2010): S220–37, esp. S220.

54 Organization for Economic Co-operation and Development (OECD), *Glossary: Humanitarian Aid* (code 070) line I.A.1.5. (2010), available at http://www.oecd.org/document/19/0,3746,en_21571361_ 39494699_39503763_1_1_1_1,00.html (viewed 4 May 2011).

55 Donini,, *Disasters*.

56 Ibid., *Disasters*, S223.

57 Stiglitz, *Globalization and Its Discontents*, 224.

58 Harvey, *Brief History*.

59 Ibid.; T. Wallace, "NGO Dilemmas: Trojan Horses for Global Neoliberalism?" *Socialist Register* 40 (2004): 202–19.

60 J.A. Leake, M.L. Kone, A.A. Yada, L.F. Barry, G. Traore, A. Ware, T. Coulibaly, A. Berthe, H. Mambu Ma Disu, N.E. Rosenstein, B.D. Plikaytis, K. Esteves, J. Kawamata, J.D. Wenger, D.L. Heymann, and B.A. Perkins, "Early Detection and Response to Meningococcal Disease Epidemics in Sub-Saharan Africa: Appraisal of the WHO Strategy," *Bulletin of the World Health Organization* 80, 5 (2002): 342–9.

61 MSF, *Management of Epidemic Meningococcal Meningitis*, 3rd ed. (Paris: Médecins Sans Frontières, 2004).

62 "Lead Poisoning in Nigeria: A Behind the Scenes Look at the Worst Lead Poisoning Outbreak on Record," *Epidemiology Monitor* (2011), available at http://www.epimonitor.net/Lead_Poisoning_In_Nigeria. htm (viewed 12 July 2011).

63 MSF, *Nigeria: MSF Helps Treat Children with Lead Poisoning.* (2010), available at http://www.doctorswithoutborders.org/news/article.cfm? id=4514&cat=field-news (viewed 4 May 2011).

64 Doyal and Pennell, *Political Economy of Health,* 43.

65 S. Chaulia, "Angola: Empire of the Humanitarians," *Journal of Humanitarian Assistance,* available at http://reliefweb.int/sites/reliefweb. int/files/resources/D55DA731ACE9F8E3C12571B20038A0FC-jha-ago-21jul.pdf (viewed 2006); Wallace, "NGO Dilemmas."

66 A.E. Ostheimer, "Aid Agencies: Providers of Essential Resources?" in *Angola's War Economy: The Role of Oil and Diamonds,* ed. J. Cilliers and C. Dietrich (Pretoria: Institute for Security Studies, 2000), 134.

67 MSF-UK, *Advocacy and témoignage,* available at http://www.msf.org. uk/advocacy.aspx (viewed 24 June 2009).

68 Patel, *Value of Nothing.*

PART TWO

Perception of the Challenges Faced
by Humanitarian Actors

4

Western Clinical Health Ethics: How Well Do They Travel to Humanitarian Contexts?

LISA SCHWARTZ, MATTHEW HUNT,
CHRIS SINDING, LAURIE ELIT,
LYNDA REDWOOD-CAMPBELL,
NAOMI ADELSON, SONYA DE LAAT,
AND JENNIFER RANFORD

HUMANITARIAN HEALTH CARE ETHICS

Humanitarian health care providers from the global North face ethical challenges that are both similar to and distinct from those they encounter in their home contexts. They are distinct because of the complexities of needs encountered in disaster, conflict, and development settings. It stands to reason that the ethical values that help guide their work must also be similar to and distinct from those employed in their home contexts.

We conducted an empirical study to examine Canadian health care providers' experiences of ethical challenges. Our study, described in more detail elsewhere,[1] consists of in-depth qualitative interviews with twenty respondents, including nurses, doctors, and other health care professionals. We asked them to describe the ethical challenges they encountered while they worked in contexts of disaster and deprivation. The respondents had a range of field experience in various countries in Africa,

Asia, and South America (as well as other places) and had participated in between one to twelve missions, with the average number's being four.[2] The results from this inquiry demonstrate that
ethical challenges have implications for the personal and professional identity of respondents and that these challenges emerge
from four main sources: (1) resource scarcity; (2) historical, political, social, and commercial structures; (3) aid agency policies and
agendas; and (4) norms associated with health professionals'
roles and interactions.[3]

As a matter of practice, many aid organizations offer pre-
departure training that covers a number of critical areas, including health and safety, cultural information, and other subjects
relevant to the place and type of work with which aid workers
will engage.[4] However, our preliminary investigations and findings indicate that humanitarian health care providers are offered
little or no formal preparation that would enable them to address
and manage ethical challenges and the moral distress they may
encounter during field missions.[5] Queries of aid organizations,
information from the interviews in our study, and the general
literature indicate little or no specific ethics-related training prior
to departure for fieldwork. As correspondence from one of the
NGOs indicated: "We do not have any training or preparation
material in the subjects that you mention" (personal correspondence). According to one respondent: "But ethical issues have
actually never ... I've never actually attended any pre-departure
sessions that talked about ethics."

Published materials on the MSF website indicate that it is not
that ethics is considered irrelevant but, rather, that health professionals are expected to draw upon the ethical codes, education,
and guidance of professional licensing bodies in their home countries: "Members undertake to respect their professional code of
ethics."[6] Apparently, it is hoped that this background and training
will provide a sufficiently firm foundation for responding to ethical issues encountered in humanitarian health care practice. Further discussion and consideration is warranted regarding whether
and how these codes are appropriate for international humanitarian work in settings characterized by resource scarcity, complex
need, and low security.

WILL ETHICS TRAVEL?

Another aid organization with which we corresponded wrote: "Health professionals are guided by their training and the requirements of their licensing boards for their ethical behaviour" (personal correspondence). So, while this organization affirms the importance of sound ethical behaviour on the part of its members, it also seems to assume that ethical standards and regulations are generalizable across contexts and that diverse national and cultural settings are similar enough to ensure that the ethical guidance provided by their licensing boards will still pertain.

Our study arose out of deep-seated concerns about these assumptions. First, being transplanted from a familiar context can affect one's means of dealing with difficult moral situations by reducing *access* to the resources and consensus upon which one normally draws. Moreover, transplantation could reduce the *applicability* of the resources and consensus upon which one normally relies. If so, then when transplanted to new clinical, social, political, and cultural contexts, health care providers will have difficulty applying the experiences and training regarding ethical practice that they received in their home country. Because ethical relativism may slide down a slippery slope into extreme divergence and, ultimately, solipsism, we wanted to examine what does and does not remain constant for health care ethics outside familiar care contexts. What we found is that, while many ethical principles and values remain constant, the ways in which they are prioritized do not. What is clear is that individuals feel ill-prepared to manage this reordering and to adapt to unfamiliar principles and morally irresolvable situations.

PRIORITIES ARE REARRANGED

Clinical ethics in Canada is mostly guided by professional codes of ethics informed by face-to-face interactions between professionals and patients. These conditions promote individual-oriented, and even patient-directed, care. Under ordinary circumstances, such an approach tends to be quite distant from the exigencies of community-oriented health care choices and rationing, at least to the extent that the latter are not directly related to individual patient care and treatment choices. So clinical ethics has traditionally focused on the best interests of an individual patient, and the cases most discussed tend to revolve around withdrawal of treatment at the end of life, debates about a woman's right to abortion, appropriate application of new and expensive health technologies, and/or whether a child of thirteen can give informed consent for treatment. In humanitarian aid situations, however, the conditions are greatly changed and the extreme need, limited resources, and uncertainties (both clinical and contextual) all mean that decision making is oriented towards rationing and that community good is related to, for example, infection control or other public health measures. Farmer and Campos argue that bioethics largely ignores the needs and concerns of the global poor, who, due to barriers to care, may not even have the chance to become "patients."[7] Many of the stories respondents told describe conflicts between patients with equal need for scarce resources and conflicts between the health of an individual patient and the health of communities. Thus, priorities may be rearranged and the values that inform decision making may be altered to reflect this. Significantly, these rearrangements are made at the proverbial bedside, and they are made not just by policy makers and managers but also by Western-trained health care practitioners. In their home settings, clinicians are taught not to engage in bedside rationing; while in the settings related to humanitarian aid work, bedside rationing might be essential and a daily part of their responsibilities. This is a clear case in which Western ethics training might not be relevant. As one humanitarian health worker put it: "You know ... maybe things can be deeply rooted that we just don't understand. And if we don't understand that, then how are we to judge them I suppose."

REPORTS OF MORAL DISTRESS

Whether it was because they were unprepared for the rearrangements in their priorities or because they had their ideals and expectations thwarted by circumstances outside their control, respondents felt an impact on their personal and professional identities. One respondent said that, for many humanitarian health care providers, moral distress was "the biggest personal morbidity associated with this kind of work – which is psychological." Another respondent described her sense of isolation and having no adequate resources to address ethical challenges: "When you're there … It's brutal. It's you and the issue you're facing."

According to Marilyn McHarg, director general of MSF Canada, in an interview on CBC Radio's *Metro Morning*,[8] an estimated 50 percent of health workers who travel with MSF will not return to do a second mission. We acknowledge that there may be many reasons for this high attrition rate. If even a small number do not return due to experiences of frustration and disillusionment related to ethical challenges, then it is possible that ethics-related preparation and support could enable these people to sustain their humanitarian health work. In order to contribute to this goal we thought it would be beneficial to generate an inventory of the types of ethical challenges reported by humanitarian health care providers who work with people in contexts of disaster, poverty, and conflict. One thing our study clearly reveals is that traditional professional ethics training is insufficient for addressing all the ethical challenges faced in the field. Further, in some cases, the expectations that accompany traditional Western professional health care ethics may even be the source of ethical tensions.

Can't Treat Everyone

It comes as no great surprise that, for respondents, resource scarcity was one of the four main causes of ethical challenges (we offer a detailed analysis of the content of these issues elsewhere).[9] They struggled deeply with the knowledge that, in their home countries, resources may be an issue of ethical debate but that, in the field, the type of care that, at home, was expected as a basic entitlement was not even available. They knew what needed to be done clinically, but they also realized that limited resources meant that they could not do it. And so needs went unmet. Respondents reported feeling powerless to provide adequate care

for the people they came to assist, but they also recognized that
they had to make choices that involved using those resources that
were available as best as they could:

> I could accept that there was a valid reason for not doing it
> [i.e., providing HIV treatment]. You know, it didn't make me
> feel any better. I felt so helpless, but ... [the agency] can't end
> up providing HIV treatment everywhere in the world. Because
> in the end that would be all they did, because it could con-
> sume the whole organization, the whole resources, every-
> thing. And so none of the other health problems would be
> addressed. So I can see it. Much as I didn't like it, I
> accepted it.

The above quotation illustrates that, because limited resources
cannot be stretched to meet even the basic needs of all those who
are suffering, tragic choices have to be made.[10] Even if there had
been a way to direct all of the organization's available resources
towards treating HIV and AIDS, this would still not have enabled
aid workers to treat all those with the disease; and, of course, it
would mean taking resources away from the treatment of other
health issues, such as TB, meningitis, and malaria. In scenarios like
this, treatment is not provided because the resources are not available over time, and, in order to be effective and to minimize the
risk of drug resistance, TB and HIV medications need to be administered over time. Learning to accept this reality on a global level
is difficult, but it is all the more challenging when a particular
person comes to seek help from a particular health provider and
has to be turned away.[11] Respondents could not provide the care
they knew was needed, and this affected their sense of self as health
professionals and humanitarians. As one respondent put it: "Going
as a doctor you know people expect you to look in their throats
and listen to their chests, but if you don't have medicines to treat
whatever you find, it puts you in an awkward situation, right?"

Respondents felt that they could not just be present as care
providers but, rather, that their roles extended to their being
judges and gate keepers of access to care – roles with which they
felt uneasy and were ill-prepared to take on. One respondent

described how she had collected donations before travelling so that she would have funds to help families obtain equipment and resources for long-term rehabilitation:

> I wanted to use money as a way of helping, but it really made my power differential a lot more pronounced than it had been previously ... For the families with children with disabilities who were going to the centre were getting help – which wasn't very much. Other families wondered why they weren't also receiving the same ... I was this person who was judging people to be worthy or not worthy. And their obvious embarrassment and gratitude ...

Allocating limited resources was a recurrent challenge for clinicians. Although such decisions were sometimes taken at the level of organizations, respondents struggled when headquarters' rationale seemed not to make much sense in relation to the local reality of a particular project. In other cases, respondents had to make micro-level allocation choices. These scenarios were a prominent source of moral uncertainty and challenge.

Social Context

Respondents were also challenged by cultural norms and expectations that were not consistent with the ethical expectations they had developed while providing care in their home settings or that were incompatible with their personal values. Many went into the field with the express intention of being sensitive to cultural differences and respectful of the norms of the community they came to assist. They expressed a strong desire to avoid succumbing to neocolonialist attitudes that create clashes between cultures and expectations. Nevertheless, despite this wariness, respondents struggled with determining how much to yield to what they believed were unethical expectations or practices: "It was, 'the men are the ones who we need so the men go first to surgery.' It was very, very difficult ... and that was very difficult on the surgeons as well, because they had no say in who was to go into surgery first."

Ethical and cultural relativism are double-edged concepts: they invite respect, tolerance, and even acceptance between cultures, but they also make it difficult to question or criticize. For participants who recognized the limitations of their understanding of a new culture, and who were conscious of wanting to avoid imposing on or dominating the host culture, this was an especially trying circumstance and one that allowed little time or opportunity to engage in debates about the finer points of comparative norms. As one respondent said:

> I know what the ethical framework is in Canada, and we are taught that in medical school and in the situation of HIV disclosure; I understand about autonomy and the privacy we place on that ... whereas when I am in the developing world I have to rely on the nature of that culture or country and I have to explicitly ask what is appropriate here or what is expected and very much rely on their advice about how to proceed.

There were also cases in which health practitioners took the "opportunity" of being outside of their usual social contexts to enact values that they knew would be unacceptable at home. In one example, a nurse was assisting when an expatriate surgeon took the opportunity to perform a tubal ligation on an unconscious woman who was undergoing unrelated abdominal surgery. The woman had not given her consent for the tubal ligation and the nurse was shocked when her attempts to advocate for the patient failed and the surgeon proceeded on the grounds that the patient had appeared emotionally unstable when she was admitted. So it would seem that not all humanitarian health care workers are cautious about imposing their views within a foreign context, and this may have with grim consequences.

A Decision Made Elsewhere

Respondents reported that aid agency policies and agendas were an additional source of ethical challenge. They often described circumstances related to vertical programs, in which their mandate (and often their agreement with local officials) for being in a particular locale restricted the conditions they could treat and the patients to whom they could provide care. While they expressed understanding and a certain relief at the obvious need for restrictions to what a single person, project, or team could do, they also felt that they were letting down those people who were excluded based on vertical program criteria. Respondents described their frustration at having to tell a mother that they could not treat her dying child because the project was simply not mandated to provide such care. Again, sometimes the remit of the team was to treat injuries related to a natural disaster, so people with illnesses and injuries unconnected to that event had to be turned away.

Some respondents were reassured by the fallback explanation that such refusals were neither their choice nor under their control. It was reassuring to be able to say that the aid agency had constructed the program and that decisions rested with the agency decision makers, usually based far away. Still, while this may have gone some way towards explaining matters, it left respondents feeling frustrated and powerless:

> I felt relieved that the decision, that I could say that the, I didn't make the decision. I'm just communicating the decision. The decision in fact was made by our country manager and they had an important meeting and they sat down and they talked about it ... to show that we're taking it seriously. So my thinking was to first use that as an anchor ... to give me a bit of confidence in the decision. But then I would also remember that I'm hundreds of miles away in this dusty, dry, hot camp and I'm the only person working with these community health workers and this other Ministry of Health nurse and that, ultimately, that's in my hands. And that's how they saw it. They wouldn't accept the argument that it's the country management team that's making the decisions.

Pushing Limits: Personal and Resource

Norms and expectations around professional roles and interactions yielded ethical challenges in the field. In certain situations respondents found themselves having to go beyond their professional fields of practice. In such cases they recognized that the needs of the situation presented a choice between acting outside their registered competencies and providing no care at all. Where they felt sufficiently competent to do so, they would provide what care they could. A general surgeon asserted: "If a woman is in obstructed labour and there is nobody else to help, I'll do a caesarean section. But you know, I prefer not to because I'm not an obstetrician and I'm not very comfortable doing it."

In another setting, a gynaecological surgeon reported:

> So, after the cyclone hit in [name of country], I was the only person who could crack an abdomen. Now, here I'm trained to do obstetrics and GYNE ... but I'm the only one who can deal with bowel perforations, typhoid, cholera, and I'm not trained for any of this. I'm operating on kids, I'm operating on men, I'm thrown into a whole bunch of circumstances where I have to make a decision whether I'm going to operate or not, and knowing if I don't, the person's going to die. In many circumstances, I'm reading a book before I'm opening a belly. So, the ethical dilemma ... is [that,] in this culture, you have resources to deal with those situations[,] with consults and stuff, but there I have to make a decision – which is the better of two bad options: having the wrong surgeon operate, or not operating and dying?

In other stories, respondents describe how cultural norms and expectations affected how they interacted with local colleagues and how they could provide care. In some settings prognoses must not be shared with patients because it is believed they will lose hope, while in other places family and community members seemed prepared to accept a death long before the aid team was ready to do so. Still other stories indicate that hierarchies between professionals in the local system made it impossible for other professionals to question certain diagnoses and treatment decisions.

Here again, respondents were conscious of imposing their own expectations, so some found opportunities to ask questions in less formal settings. They said that talking with local health providers and fellow expatriates helped them to gain a perspective on issues and to understand the origins of professional differences. Others said that, due to the brevity of their stays in a community, they never had the chance to do this. They indicated, with some regret, that they had left before a decision had been worked out and did not know how things had turned out for the patient.

The context in which humanitarian health care is provided contributes to shaping ethical considerations. Resources are scarcer, needs higher, and expectations differ from those made by the health providers' countries of origin. Members of aid organizations clearly have a genuine desire to behave in the interests of their patients, especially given that they recognize the severity of the consequences of not providing treatment for patients who have few if any alternatives for care. However, respondents indicated that, in at least some circumstances, professional norms interfered with their ability to help.

WHEN RESPONDING TO NEEDS

Generally speaking, respondents related stories about ethical challenges that led them to question professional boundaries and expectations. When, if ever, is it okay to work outside one's professional limits or at the margins of one's capacities? When, if ever, is it okay to work outside agency agendas and project mandates? Once you start providing care, what is your duty to continue? How, when resources are insufficient for all who need care, can we ethically choose which patients receive care? Who should be involved in such decisions? How can we live with our (personal and professional) selves when we deny needed care? Are we contributing to government inaction by providing care that is the responsibility of local governments? When and how can projects be ended in an ethically justified manner? Where will I draw the line? Each of these is an important ethical question with implications for ethical interactions with patients and host communities. That providers are struggling with these issues is an indication that they need support to help them reflect on the

ethical experiences associated with humanitarian work. Ultimately, the patients and communities they serve deserve the kind
of ethical consideration that examines and explores available
options in a local context.

AID AGENCIES AND ETHICAL DEBATE

Recent activities have demonstrated that aid organizations valorize
reflection on their practice, and this includes ethical analysis. The
Perceptions Conference is a good example of this commitment,
"inviting participants, ranging from various NGOs to academia[,]
to discuss current perceptions, realities, and future humanitarian
challenges," including ethics in humanitarian action.[12] Discussion
examines a range of topics, from security to organizational
culture and the professionalization of humanitarian health care.

Opening spaces for ethical exploration is important for aid
agencies as discussion is the best way to help to identify and to
address ethical concerns and, where possible, to create a consensus base for deliberating upon and (one hopes) resolving ethical
challenges. Creating space for ethics is important in pre-departure
planning and training, for reflection and conflict resolution in the
field, and also for debriefing and long-term support after missions. Also, ethical considerations can help to support policy
setting and revision, such as priority setting at the NGO level.

According to one respondent: "In the name of ethics, you can
challenge medical policies. You can challenge, which is great, but,
I mean, it takes a lot of courage." Such courage can be strength-
ened through training and creating a culture that not only permits
but also invites the identification of ethical dimensions of health
care practice in humanitarian aid.[13]

RESOURCES

There are multiple resources that could help aid organizations to
inspire, train, and apply the ethics of humanitarian health care
practice. In the first instance, organizational statements help
make the organization's values explicit. Making mission statements public invites support and debate about what values ought

to guide the work and how they could best be played out. Inter-organization value statements can also be a source of guidance with regard to values and humanitarian action (e.g., International Federation of the Red Cross Code of Conduct;[14] Humanitarian Charter of the Sphere Project).[15]

As part of education and pre-departure training, cases for discussion are acknowledged as the best means of learning ethical theory and/or standards in ways that help to inspire imagination, model debate about ethical issues,[16] and provide an opportunity to learn how to seek support. We have begun to develop these and further resources, such as a humanitarian health ethics analysis model;[17] *Ethics of Engaged Presence*, a framework of values and orientations to support ethical practice in humanitarian work; workshops for pre-departure training and professional development; and on-line resources that are available wherever humanitarian health workers have access to the internet. It is important not to underestimate the value of resources ready to hand, such as the support to be gained from just talking with colleagues about ethical challenges that arise during field missions.[18] Crucially, local resources, such as colleagues and community members, can make excellent informants and models that may help to clarify ethical norms and the origins of disparities.

KEY QUESTIONS ON MOTIVATIONS AND EXPECTATIONS

Reflection is a useful tool in any kind of clinical practice. One key point for reflection concerns the expectations and realities of the different actors involved in a particular enterprise and in a given context. Motivations and expectations are important influences on the experiences of health care providers in humanitarian work. Overly idealized motivations, or mismatched expectations between different actors, can be a source of disillusionment or diminished effectiveness.[19] In assessing one's participation, it may be helpful for humanitarian health care practitioners to ask the following questions:

• What are my goals?
• What are the goals of the organization that is sending me?

- What does the patient need?
- What does the community need?
- Who determines these? Do they harmonize?

It is important to examine the potentially divergent answers to these questions because a lack of harmonization between any or all of them immediately creates an ethical dilemma/challenge – one that, potentially, could be overcome with proper attention and reordering (or at least recognized and addressed).

Finally, there is increasing discussion about the possibility of professionalizing humanitarian health care practice.[20] This is a proposal that requires careful examination. Regardless of whether or not professionalization is desirable, clearly a more considered attitude towards humanitarian health care practice would produce some worthwhile elements: increased clarity of ethical values for practitioners and transparency of ethical standards and expectations, to name only two. Regardless of the outcome of this debate, creating a space for ethics in the day-to-day practice of humanitarian health care could not only improve responsiveness to the communities with which humanitarian health care providers engage but also support the providers themselves.

NOTES

1 L. Schwartz, C. Sinding, M. Hunt, L. Elit, L. Redwood-Campbell, N. Adelson, J. Ranford, and S. De Laat, "Ethics in Humanitarian Aid Work: Learning from the Narratives of Humanitarian Health Workers," *American Journal of Bioethics: Primary Research* 1, 3 (2010): 45–54.

2 Funding for the study was obtained from the Canadian Institutes of Health Research (CIHR), and it was approved by the McMaster University Research Ethics Board.

3 Schwartz, "Ethics in Humanitarian Aid Work."

4 M. McCall and P. Salama, "Selection, Training and Support of Relief Workers: An Occupational Health Issue," *British Medical Journal* 318 (1999): 113–16 ; R.T. Moresky, M.J. Eliades, M.A. Bhimani,

E.B. Bunney, and M.J. VanRooyen, "Preparing International Relief Workers for Health Care in the Field: An Evaluation of Organizational Practices," *Prehospital and Disaster Medicine* 16, 4 (2001): 257–62.

5 A. De Waal, *Famine Crimes: Politics and the Disaster Relief Industry in Africa* (Indiana: Indiana University Press, 1998); A. De Waal, "The Humanitarians' Tragedy: Escapable and Inescapable Cruelties," *Disasters* 34 (2010): S137; J. Sheather and T. Shah, "Ethical Dilemmas in Medical Humanitarian Practice: Cases for Reflection from Médecins Sans Frontières," *Journal of Medical Ethics* 37 (2011): 162–5; H.L. Zielinski, *Health and Humanitarian Concerns: Principles and Ethics* (Leiden: Sitjhoff, 1994).

6 MSF Charter, available at http://www.msf.ca/about-msf/msf-charter/.

7 P. Farmer and N. Gastineau Campos, "Rethinking Medical Ethics: A View from Below," *Dev World Bioethics* 4, 1 (2004): 17–41.

8 M. McHarg, *Metro Morning* (Toronto), CBC Radio, 25 January 2010.

9 C. Sinding, L. Schwartz, M. Hunt, L. Redwood-Campbell, L. Elit, and J. Ranford, "'Playing God Because You Have To': Canadian Health Professionals' Narratives of Rationing Care in Humanitarian and Development Work," *Public Health Ethics* 3, 2 (2010): 89–90.

10 B. Williams, "Conflicts of Values," in *Moral Luck* (Cambridge: Cambridge University Press, 1981).

11 D. Devakumar, "Cholera and Nothing More," *Public Health Ethics* 3, 1 (2010): 53–4.

12 Available at http://www.msf.ca/themes/msf-perceptions-conference/ (viewed April 2012).

13 N. Ford, R. Zachariah, E. Mills, and R. Upshur, "Defining the Limits of Emergency Humanitarian Action: Where, and How, to Draw the Line?" *Public Health Ethics* 1–4 (2009); S. Hurst, N. Mezger, and A. Mauron, "Allocating Resources in Humanitarian Medicine," *Public Health Ethics* 2, 1 (2009): 89–99.

14 IFRC (International Federation of Red Cross and Red Crescent Societies), "The Code of Conduct for the International Red Cross and Red Crescent Movement and NGOs," in *Disaster Relief* (Geneva: IFRC, 1994).

15 Sphere Project, "The Humanitarian Charter and Minimum Standards," in *Disaster Response*, 2011, available at http://www.sphereproject.org/ content/view/720/200/lang,english/ (viewed 5 August 2011).

16 J. Goldie, L. Schwartz, A. McConnachie, B. Jolly, and J. Morrison, "Can Students' Reasons for Choosing Set Answers to Ethical Vignettes Be Reliably Rated? Development and Testing of a Method," *Medical Teacher* 26, 8 (2004): 713–18.

17 M.R. Hunt, "Establishing Moral Bearings: Ethics and Expatriate Health Care Professionals in Humanitarian Work," *Disasters* 35, 3 (2011): 606–22.

18 M.R. Hunt, "Moral Experience of Canadian Health Care Professionals in Humanitarian Work," *Prehospital and Disaster Medicine* 24, 6 (2009): 518–24.

19 M.R. Hunt and R. Matthew, "Resources and Constraints for Addressing Ethical Issues in Medical Humanitarian Work: Experiences of Expatriate Healthcare Professionals," *American Journal of Disaster Medicine* 4, 5: (2009): 261–71.

20 See Johnson (chapter 6, this volume).

5

Programming, Footprints, and Relationships: The Link between Perceptions and Humanitarian Security

LARISSA FAST[1]

After the December 2007 Algiers bombing that killed seventeen UN personnel from various agencies, the UN ordered an investigation into the attack in order to identify lessons learned. Among other things, the investigation revealed an image problem, which UN personnel attributed to a widespread perception of the UN as effecting a "pro-Western" or "anti-Muslim" agenda. This image, in turn, hinders their work and threatens their security.[2] In Afghanistan, the perceived affiliation of some aid agencies with the allied political and military agenda put their national staff at risk during "coordinated assassination campaigns."[3] While perceptions can prove deadly in some cases, in others they are seemingly more innocuous.

Community perceptions of aid workers often rely upon what people see aid workers and aid organizations do, and vice versa. Thus, when community members see aid workers driving around in costly Landrovers, eating in nice restaurants, and living in large, guarded compounds without a direct and visible benefit to themselves, they might conclude that aid workers enjoy privileges at the expense of funds and resources that should be destined for their communities and families. Likewise, when aid workers repeatedly encounter individuals bent on manipulating the system, profiting from bribes, or benefitting from the diversion of aid supplies, they might be more likely to tar others with the same brushstrokes. Aid workers and communities perceive each other differently, but both their perceptions are mutually influential and elicit multiple potential consequences.

With regard to humanitarian and aid work, there are two practical reasons for examining perceptions: (1) because doing so improves the delivery and effectiveness of humanitarian and aid programs, which could shape system reform; and (2) because how communities and other stakeholders perceive aid organizations is intimately connected to security. This chapter focuses primarily on the latter, examining the "acceptance" approach to security management and the role of perception in gaining and maintaining consent for an organization's presence and work. I draw upon research conducted in South Sudan in April 2011 as part of a collaborative project researching acceptance as an approach to NGO security management,[4] and I suggest three interrelated themes with regard to perceptions and their effect on humanitarian security.

PERCEPTIONS AND ACCEPTANCE AS A SECURITY MANAGEMENT STRATEGY

The connection between security and perceptions is most apparent with regard to positing acceptance as a security management strategy. Acceptance is "founded on effective relationships and cultivating and maintaining consent from beneficiaries, local authorities, belligerents, and other stakeholders. This in turn is a means of reducing or removing potential threats in order to access vulnerable populations and undertake programme activities."[5] Acceptance, therefore, is not only a matter of addressing existing threats in order to protect staff but also of ensuring access and enabling programming. As a security management strategy, it contrasts with "protection," which relies on mechanisms to "harden" the organization and its staff and resources as targets, and "deterrence," which aims to prevent attacks through the use of counter-threats such as withdrawal or armed escort.[6]

Given the dynamic nature of the contexts in which aid agencies operate, agencies must continuously seek, monitor, and maintain acceptance over time and across locations. At its most basic level, acceptance is akin to tolerance, with an organization's being tolerated because it provides much needed services. In this case, community members and other stakeholders give tacit or explicit consent to the organization's presence and work. Higher levels of acceptance often involve community actions on behalf of an organization, either to prevent an incident or to assist in dealing with the aftermath of an incident. Because acceptance builds on relationships that confer consent, it is by nature very localized. Acceptance gained in one location or with one group does not necessarily transfer to neighbouring locations or groups. Despite being localized, acceptance is not gained in a vacuum, and global events may disrupt or challenge whatever acceptance an organization may have. When, in late September 2005, the Danish newspaper *Jyllands-Posten* published cartoons that many Muslims found offensive, throughout the world many agencies with Danish, Christian, or even Western affiliations experienced a backlash, regardless of the goodwill and degree of security they might have previously enjoyed.

Thinking of acceptance as both dynamic and tenuous forces a deliberate dismantling of the concept in order to more closely examine its component parts.[7] First, agencies adopting an acceptance strategy must ask themselves from whom acceptance or consent is needed, who is accepted, and who works to gain acceptance. At a minimum, aid agencies must seek formal consent from national governments and local authorities, often in the form of a Memorandum of Understanding, to operate in a country. Likewise, at a minimum, they seek tacit consent for their presence and activities from belligerents, beneficiaries, and members of the communities in which they work. Each of these groups (and others, like local business leaders) is likely to harbour different perceptions of an NGO based on the quality and nature of its relationship with the agency and how it is affected by it. For aid agencies, mapping the perceptions of these diverse constituencies and stakeholders is an important endeavour. In particular, mapping stakeholders involves identifying and analyzing the motives, attitudes, capabilities, and relationships of actors who have the power to positively or negatively influence programs and security. Mapping the context requires attention to the environment and circumstances, with a focus on how the context and organizational values, mission, and programming interact. These mapping exercises help to identify who directly and indirectly gains or loses from the NGO's presence and activities. For instance, when agencies use and hire local suppliers they build relationships with local businesspeople, support the local economy, provide employment opportunities, and establish connections across a range of stakeholders. This, in turn, may have positive, if indirect, effects on security. On the other hand, consistently using outside or foreign suppliers, especially when local suppliers might be able to provide similar services, could generate resentment and contribute to negative perceptions of an NGO.

Even when a variety of stakeholders consent to the presence of an NGO, exactly who and what within the organization is accepted may differ. One individual who carefully cultivates relationships with local government officials may enjoy a high degree of respect and acceptance, but this acceptance may not automatically transfer to his or her successor. Likewise, acceptance for a particular individual may or may not transfer to his or her organization. Individuals may be more or less accepted because of characteristics such as ethnic background or religion, and this may differ for nationals and internationals depending on the context. Similarly, levels of acceptance for some programs, like school feeding programs or veterinary services, may be higher than that of others, like gender-based violence programming. Stakeholder acceptance for programs that meet basic and pressing needs, such as medical care or shelter, may be higher than it is for programs that provide less tangible results.

How an agency seeks to gain acceptance is context-dependent. Whether the agency is able to gain and maintain acceptance in a context is inextricably linked to multiple areas of its operations, including programs, procurement, and human resources. Thus, gaining and maintaining acceptance cannot be confined to those responsible for security management. The actions and behaviours of all staff, from program managers and administrative staff to guards, drivers, and cleaners, can influence an individual's and an organization's level of acceptance.

Second, the idea that each staff person can influence an agency's level of acceptance suggests that gaining acceptance cannot be confined only to the pursuit of effective programming. Agencies that adopt an acceptance strategy must proactively engage with various constituencies over time and account for the dynamic nature of consent and acceptance. In addition to effective and responsive programming, such proactive engagement suggests the need for a clear articulation of, and education about, the principles and mission of the organization; for in-depth understanding and analysis of the context and stakeholders; and for attention to building a broad-based network of relationships. It requires negotiating for access to populations and for effective communication to a broad constituency.

Agencies cannot simply state their principles and values; instead, they must consistently demonstrate them in practice. For some organizations in South Sudan, reaching out to and developing relationships with these other stakeholders is a key activity that informs every aspect of their programming. According to one organization, "if we've surprised anyone by being there, we're not doing our job right."[8] For these agencies, the strategy of "building relationships without preference" – a manifestation of the principle of neutrality – involves a slow and intensive process of going from village to village to explain the agency and its work. Monitoring what communities and other stakeholders say and think about aid agencies can provide important clues about levels of acceptance. These include official *and* unofficial messages, whether these surface in local or in international media and regardless of the sender's connection to the organization.

Organizations should also attend to the quality and nature of their relationships with stakeholders. In Afghanistan, in a deliberate effort to nurture the relationships and build acceptance, Mercy Corps hosted Iftahar celebrations for government and community elders to break the fast during Ramadan.[9] Identifying leaders and influential individuals in a community is part of a stakeholder analysis. Cultivating their acceptance may involve learning more about who they are, what roles they play, to whom they relate, who they influence, and by whom they are influenced. Understanding these stakeholders and their cultural context can help in negotiating access to vulnerable populations – a process that occurs at various levels. Agencies conduct formal and informal negotiations for access and presence, both with host governments and with armed guards at checkpoints. Developing relationships with all stakeholders – something that is often achieved through listening, visiting, and "drinking tea" – requires time and effort.

In contrast, a program-only based implementation of acceptance can be exclusive as it does not necessarily seek out or take into account the perceptions of those other than program beneficiaries. Clearly, the perceptions of beneficiaries are important, but equally important are the perceptions of any stakeholder who could prevent access, harm the agency's staff, or hinder its programs. Do these stakeholders understand the mission and values of the organization and why they do not benefit? This can prove decisive since otherwise they may resent the resources that others receive. In 2006 in Afghanistan, for example, Mercy Corps chose to adopt a "zero-visibility approach" to security that relied heavily on community acceptance. In doing so, Mercy Corps capitalized on its long-standing presence in the country, its "local" staff, its participatory programming, and its extensive relationships and networks in that country. It also chose to focus on an area of core competence – agricultural livelihoods – rather than to implement the more politically charged work of responding to conflict-related displacement. Mercy Corps' overall strategy proved successful, enabling it to operate in areas in which other foreign NGOs could not.[10]

The administrative policies and procedures related to staffing decisions are another critical component of acceptance, and these involve: who is hired and fired, and why; the skills and competencies of staff members; and the overall staff profile and turnover. Many organizations in South Sudan employ a combination of international (expatriates from outside Africa), regional (expatriates from East or other parts of Africa), and national (Sudanese) staff members. Of the national staff, some work in sub-offices located in or near their villages of origin, while others are "relocated" to other parts of the country, depending on the organization's needs and the person's qualifications. Such designations, while useful in an organizational context, create an internal hierarchy, with local and national staff, all Sudanese, at the "lowest grade." Some research informants suggested that these internal hierarchies (and, in some cases, the lack of local hiring) may generate resentment and lessen acceptance, especially given the generous benefits (e.g., leave policies, health insurance, and access to health facilities) and higher pay that international and some regional staff enjoy over national or local staff. In South Sudan, this was of particular concern with regard to young or inexperienced international staff members, who were seen as having equal or fewer qualifications than national staff members yet receiving higher pay and more benefits. Administrative decisions about staffing may not consider the potential security implications of benefits packages or staff hierarchies, despite the fact that this appears to be a source of friction both within organizations and between organizations and various stakeholders. In addition, the actions and behaviours of staff members, and their appropriateness or inappropriateness in a given cultural context, can affect levels of acceptance. Cultural dictates in South Sudan suggest that it is inappropriate for younger, particularly female, staff members to give instructions to elders.

Together these factors shape how various stakeholders perceive the organization. Clearly, acceptance is complex and requires attention to programming, staffing considerations, networks, relationships, and organizational identity, all of which must be seen as part of, rather than separate from, security management.

LESSONS FROM SOUTH SUDAN

Our research on the strategy of acceptance in South Sudan identified three consistent and interrelated themes, each of which builds on the others. While the findings are commonsensical in and of themselves, they also serve as reminders of the importance of paying attention to detail and the basics of human interactions, particularly with regard to their potential effect on humanitarian security. First, community perceptions of aid agencies are shaped but not wholly defined by the programs they offer. The primary way that organizations in South Sudan work to build acceptance is through their programming and services, particularly through meeting the needs of the populations they serve. In this way, many organizations and stakeholders see acceptance as needs-based: "if you give people what they need, then officials, communities accept you" (interview with beneficiary during field visit in Sudan). Timely, transparent, and relevant services and programming to meet community needs serve as a foundation for acceptance.

If meeting needs is the foundation for acceptance, the way organizations provide such services also affects community and other stakeholder perceptions. For example, the lack of tangible results or unmet promises may create negative perceptions and result in insecurity for program staff. Negative perceptions may also decrease a community's motivation to share information about actual or potential security threats. NGO staff and community members in South Sudan cited the pitfalls of needs assessments, especially repeated assessments from one or more NGOs, which can raise community expectations or be interpreted as a promise of future service delivery. Failure to deliver can generate resentment, which, in turn, negatively affects the ways that communities perceive NGOs. Likewise, delays, especially unexplained ones, can adversely affect community perceptions, as can a lack of transparency with regard to how NGOs make decisions about whom to hire, where to work, or how to spend resources.

How different stakeholders perceive organizations often reflects their own self-interests. Community members would rather that they receive assistance than that neighbouring communities do so, and government officials wish to see services in their area rather than other areas to promote a positive impression. Managing these diverse and often contradictory interests presents a challenge for aid agencies. Few organizations in South Sudan, however, deliberately and consistently integrated activities specifically designed to build acceptance into their programming strategies or into their attempts to account for perceptions; rather, they relied on timely, relevant, and responsive programming. As a result, the security implications of programming decisions and their ripple effect on perceptions are not necessarily front and centre. In places like Afghanistan, where security concerns are acute, organizations that implement an acceptance strategy likely do so with greater deliberation and systematic intent than is the case elsewhere.

A second finding is that the image that NGOs think they project is not always the image that communities and other stakeholders perceive, and this results in a perception gap. The research showed that communities are generally able to distinguish between organizations (and sometimes label them "good" or "bad") regardless of whether or not they are beneficiaries of their programs or services. Aid agencies should therefore assume that community members are paying close attention to who they are and what they do. This casts doubt on any assumption that NGOs are lumped together or seen as the same, even though distinctions may be unclear to non-beneficiary populations or to officials who do not regularly interact with aid organizations or directly benefit from their programs. In South Sudan, community members to whom we spoke were able to name which NGOs provided food, education, or water and sanitation in their communities. This type of "branding by service provided" helps an organization distinguish itself from others and, in and of itself, suggests a basic level of acceptance. If services or resources dry up or are not delivered in an acceptable manner (i.e., NGOs are expected to deliver what communities need, to do so on time, and to go through local leaders), it is conceivable that any degree of acceptance that exists will dry up. In short, this is a shallow foundation for acceptance as a security management approach. By contrast, a more robust degree of distinctiveness is present if community members are able to articulate an organization's motivating principles and values, as opposed to identifying it based on the services it provides, and give consent for the organization's presence and activities based on this vision.

Another type of perception gap is apparent from comments community members, government officials, and others expressed

about NGO resources and infrastructure (e.g., vehicles, compounds, equipment, and staff members) – the NGO's "footprint" –
and the services they deliver. The perceived disparity between the
extent of an organization's footprint and the services it provides
is a source of discontent and resentment. According to one individual: "INGO [international NGO] compounds are like islands of
comfort in the middle of want. They are eating nicely, driving nice
cars. Beyond the gates people are dying. They have the best in the
ocean ... nice food and the best cars!" In South Sudan, the perception that many NGOs hire outside of the local community adds to
the discontent and leads to calls for greater accountability and
transparency with regard to project budgets and organizational
policies. In defence of these choices, many positions require qualifications that can be hard to find among those living in rural
South Sudan as NGOs are competing for staff on an international
market that dictates pay scales and qualifications. To address this
discrepancy, one organization asks community elders and/or leaders to sit in on job interviews. After the person is hired, these
elders explain to the community who the organization hired and
why. Such efforts represent attempts to deliberately address the
perception gap.

The perception gap implies that building acceptance is not only
about what organizations provide, the programs they implement,
or what they say about their policies and procedures. What organizations do and the image they project through their footprint
in the country sends a powerful, if largely implicit, message about
their values.[11] The inequities in the system – apparent in the
resources, benefits, pay scales, and physical infrastructure of
NGOs – can be sources of envy, anger, and misunderstanding. The
programs and services that humanitarian and aid agencies offer
respond to the inequalities between those who have (or who have
access) and those who have not. At the same time, these agencies
are often visible manifestations of these inequalities. While in
many cases the perception gap will have no direct ramifications
on an organization's level of security, it is equally conceivable that
it could erode the degree of goodwill and acceptance that many

aid agencies enjoy in South Sudan and elsewhere around the world and, thus, contribute to conditions that could allow insecurity to increase for humanitarian and aid actors. An organization's vulnerability to attack may be greater if stakeholders with the capacity to do harm to the organization have no sense of what it does or why it is there. The information void is often filled with rumours and accusations. A lack of awareness of its acceptance gap has potentially negative implications for the degree of security an organization might enjoy if it took measures to address the sources of that gap.

Finally, our collaborative research in South Sudan highlights the importance of the "intangible" aspects of acceptance, which are associated with relationships, respect, and how people are treated (all of which are important factors in determining how aid workers and aid agencies are perceived). Community members and government officials in South Sudan spoke of their responsibility to ensure that NGO staff members are safe – a responsibility that was usually related to cultural notions of hospitality and the obligation to protect visitors. Yet the actions of some aid workers abrogated this protection. In particular, community members mentioned the ill treatment of women and cattle as actions that could damage this culturally engrained sense of responsibility. On the other hand, the heroic efforts of some individuals aid workers and the relationships they enjoyed with Sudanese were remembered many years later. Over twenty years later, South Sudanese fondly remember John Parker, an aid worker in the 1980s, and how he fled the bombing of South Sudanese villages alongside the villagers, risking his own life to continue to provide assistance. Villagers called the bed nets he delivered "John Parker" mosquito nets.

Though the above examples tend to be extreme, the quality of individual interactions, particularly the importance of smiling, greeting, and shaking hands when meeting people, can positively affect perceptions. Short tempers and aggressive behaviour, in contrast, are not welcome. Some Sudanese expressed the sense that outsiders – whether Sudanese from other parts of the country, regional staff, or expatriate staff – often treat community members as inferior due to their being illiterate or having less education than the foreigners. Others suggested that some NGO staff members, particularly expatriates, do not interact respectfully with government officials (as they would in their own countries). These behaviours negatively affect relationships. In general, informants indicated that courteous and respectful interactions are important if one wishes to achieve acceptance. Many NGO staff also recognized the importance of these less tangible elements of relationships with communities and other stakeholders. One informant told a story about how an expatriate staff member who arrived on a temporary assignment ruined a carefully cultivated relationship with a government official in one day. The government official perceived the expatriate's behaviour as rude and aggressive and, as a result, refused to work with the organization. The organization's level of acceptance with this government official, which had been built over months and even years, dissipated quickly as a result of individual behaviour.

NGO staff themselves often recognize the inconsistencies that exist. During the research, several informants emphasized the need for more innovative programming to ensure better acceptance. They suggested that NGOs should emphasize living with and in communities, avoid clustering residences and compounds in particular areas ("NGOs are all clustered in one place. It is like we are scared or something"), and meet with beneficiaries and community members "outside the project cycle." These informants observed that relationships with beneficiaries are often built immediately prior to projects, maintained during projects, and then end at the same time as does the granting period. As a result, they are project – or meeting-based relationships that are confined to project cycles and goals. In asking for programming that is "genuine" or "sincere," two words that community members and government officials used to describe the type of programming they would like to see, they are expressing a desire for relationships based on mutual respect. The less desirable alternative, it seems, is instrumentalized and hierarchical relationships that are based on transactions between givers and receivers.

CONCLUSION

An NGO using a vehicle that was not well marked was attacked in an eastern state in South Sudan, despite its having an armed escort. The attackers took all the money and cell phones. The NGO recovered all items except the money, primarily through the intervention of one of the villages in which it worked. Unsolicited, the villagers sought out and found the perpetrators. They encouraged the NGO to press charges and served as witnesses at the trial. The actions of the community on behalf of the NGO suggest that it enjoyed a significant level of acceptance in that community. Clearly, acceptance can produce important security dividends. However, it does not come automatically; rather, agencies must continuously seek, monitor, and maintain acceptance.

An acceptance approach to security management implies that aid agencies should examine the perceptions of any actor with the capacity to negatively affect the organization, not only those with whom they interact on a regular basis. Implementing an acceptance approach requires attention to detail, from decisions about staffing and the physical location and profile of offices and compounds to how individual staff members interact with community members and others, whether at project sites or checkpoints. It should be deliberate, extending beyond programming and program staff to include all staff members, from cleaners to drivers. Thus, while effective and responsive programming is important, agencies choosing to implement an acceptance approach must realize that their program, footprint, and image are integral to how they are perceived and, ultimately, to the degree of their security.

NOTES

1   Although I am author of this chapter, I draw extensively on my work on the Collaborative Learning Approach to NGO Security Management (CLANSM) project, funded by the US Agency for International Development, for the examples and conclusions herein. I am indebted to my

colleagues Michael O'Neill, Elizabeth Rowley, and Faith Freeman as this chapter reflects some of our collective insights and ideas, all of which have emerged as a result of the project. This chapter draws upon field research conducted in South Sudan by my colleagues and me in April 2011 (see also endnote 4) and that was part of this project. Any errors, omissions, or misrepresentations, however, are my own.

2 Independent Panel, "'Towards a Culture of Security and Accountability': The Report of the Independent Panel on Safety and Security of UN Personnel and Premises Worldwide," New York, United Nations, *Brahimi Report*, 9 June 2008, p. 70, available at http://www.un.org/News/dh/infocus/terrorism/PanelOnSafetyReport.pdf (viewed 5 March 2009).

3 N. Pont, "Southern Afghanistan: Acceptance Still Works," *Humanitarian Exchange*, 6–9 January 2011, p. 6, available at http://www.odihpn.org/report.asp?id=3178 (viewed 20 July 2011).

4 The research examined the acceptance approach and, more specifically, the questions of how NGOs implement an acceptance approach to security management at the field level, how they monitor and assess the presence and degree of acceptance, and whether it is effective. My South Sudan team members included: Reginold Patterson (Save the Children), Alfred Amule (Catholic Relief Services), Simon Bonis (Mercy Corps), Lasu Joseph (Norwegian Refugee Council), Anthony Kollie (American Refugee Committee), James Luer Gach Diew (Sudanese Red Crescent), Sirocco Mayom Biar Atek (BRAC), Chris Nyamandi (ACT Alliance), and Jimmy Okumu (Nonviolent Peaceforce). For more about the project and findings from South Sudan, Uganda, and Kenya, visit http://www.acceptanceresearch.org (see also note 1).

5 L. Fast and M. O'Neill, "A Closer Look at Acceptance," *Humanitarian Exchange*, 3–6 June 2010, 5–6, available at http://www.odihpn.org/report.asp?id=3116 (viewed 4 August 2011).

6 HPN, "Operational Security Management in Violent Environments," *Good Practice Review* 8 (London, UK: Humanitarian Practice Network, ODI, revised December 2010), available at http://www.odihpn.org/report.asp?id=3159 (viewed 16 December 2010).

7 See L. Fast, F. Freeman, M. O'Neill, and E. Rowley, "In Acceptance We Trust? Conceptualizing Acceptance as a Viable Approach to Security

Management," *Disasters* (forthcoming) for a more in-depth discussion of this conceptualization of acceptance.

8 All quotations, unless otherwise indicated, are from field research conducted in South Sudan in April 2011 and reported in Larissa Fast, Reginold Patterson, Alfred Amule, Simon Bonis, Lasu Joseph, Anthony Kollie, James Luer Gach Diew, Sirocco Mayom Biar Atek, Chris Nyamandi, and Jimmy Okumu, *South Sudan Country Report: Key Findings from Field Research on Acceptance in South Sudan* (Washington, DC: Save the Children, 2011).

9 Pont, "Southern Afghanistan," 7.

10 Ibid., 6–8.

11 M.B Anderson, *Do No Harm: How Aid Can Support Peace – or War* (Boulder, CO: Lynne Rienner, 1999).

6

Professionalizing Humanitarian Action

KIRSTEN JOHNSON

RATIONALE

The need for the professionalization of the humanitarian sector is widely recognized and the mechanisms for how such an association might be formed and how it might operate are being discussed at international meetings attended by, among others, academics, practitioners, humanitarian organizations, the UN, and the private sector. This chapter explores the concept of a professional humanitarian association and presents some ideas regarding how such an association could be developed by making use of examples from other fields. It concludes with recommendations for moving forward.

Despite the advances of the humanitarian sector in building evidence-based training and service delivery, humanitarian intervention remains uncoordinated and ad hoc. Recently, the Inter-Agency Standing Committee (IASC) evaluated the response to the humanitarian crisis in Haiti in January 2010,[1] and it highlighted critical issues pertaining to humanitarian workers that hindered the quality of the initial response.[2] These issues included a majority of inexperienced, small NGOs and humanitarian workers who lacked a professional approach to and knowledge of the situation; a limited understanding of the Haitian context; insufficient communication with the local population; an inability to consolidate and report information; and lack of assistance to better support coping strategies. The challenges arising from the Haiti response are not new, and they produce a number of questions relevant to the selection, training, certification, and professionalization of humanitarian service providers.

There has been a move to enhance quality and accountability on the part of organizations that assist or act on behalf of people affected by disasters, conflict, poverty, or other crises. Initiatives focused on enhancing the quality of service delivery and accountability in the humanitarian sector include: the Sphere Project;[3] Livestock Emergency Guidelines and Standards (LEGS);[4] the Humanitarian Accountability Partnership International (HAP-I);[5] the Active Learning Network for Accountability and Performance in Humanitarian Action (ALNAP);[6] People in Aid;[7] the Good Enough Guide by the Emergency Capacity Building Project (ECB);[8] the Compass Method by Groupe Urgence, Réhabilitation, Développement (URD);[9] the Synergie Qualité guide by Coordination Solidarité, Urgence, Développement (SUD);[10] The Inter-Agency Network for Education in Emergencies (INEE);[11] and national self-regulatory schemes in the non-profit sector. For the most part, these initiatives focus on accountability from an organizational, systems, and management perspective. People in Aid and the Sphere Project provide codes of conduct for humanitarian workers, but none provides either a mechanism to ensure individual adherence to the code(s) of conduct or disciplinary action for violations or misconduct in the field. Furthermore, there is no official body that offers protection, access to standardized training, and education and strategies for networking to individuals who are career humanitarians.

As the world experiences larger, more frequent emergencies due to changing demographics and issues around climate change and urbanization (among others), there will be an increased demand for humanitarian action and a greater need for trained and experienced humanitarians. Already the sector is experiencing rapid growth. Global staffing levels are rising at an average annual rate of 6 percent, and there is now a total population of roughly

210,800 humanitarian workers in the field.[12] However, attrition levels are as high as 25 to 45 percent, and training resources are only 1 percent of overall budgets per year, possibly partly accounting for the high attrition rates.[13] A recent survey by Enhancing Learning and Research for Humanitarian Assistance (ELRHA) shows that 92 percent of field-based humanitarian workers are national staff.[14] The national staffs in humanitarian organizations are overwhelmingly looking to enhance their own training and professional standing. Sixty percent of respondents answered that they had done some sort of professional development training in the last twelve months, and 67 percent of these said that they wanted a professional association. Given that the majority of humanitarian service providers are national staffs who come from Southern countries, the demand for better and more accessible (i.e., local) opportunities for training and professional recognition of qualifications will increase. At present most master's-level programs are based in the North and are prohibitively expensive. Having a system that recognizes another model for professional development outside of the master's-level certification would enhance the legitimacy of Southern practitioners (who cannot gain access to such programs) by allowing them access to other opportunities for training and certification. Furthermore, having a professional association that offers support and training resources designed for national staff from the South would contribute to a more sustainable human resource pool (with less turnover) as well as to the conservation of some its most experienced and valued members.

At present there are an estimated one hundred master's programs in humanitarian action worldwide that produce approximately five thousand graduates per year. The Network of Humanitarian Assistance (NOHA) International Association of Universities has graduated over two thousand master's in humanitarian assistance since its program began in 1993.[15] There are another eight to ten university-based diploma programs in humanitarian studies. The majority of all the programs are in France, followed by Switzerland, with the rest being in Europe and North America. These academic programs are intended to produce leaders and experts in humanitarian action. However, there are no core curricula, there is no sharing of course materials, there are no established standards, and no program accreditation is in place. What is being taught to these students is largely based on what the instructor is able to teach and is often far from the practical needs of the field. It could be argued that the courses in many of the programs are not field-informed or evidence-based but, rather, are based on the discipline and expertise of the initiator. Evidence to support this conclusion is provided when one looks at the list of topics in the syllabi, which focus on socio-anthropology, law, economics, public affairs, and public health. A professional association that is involved with the creation of core curricula and the accreditation of academic programs and teachers, using internal and external peer review, would provide quality assurance, enhance the evidence base, and standardize the educational content of all the programs that are currently certifying graduates and the future leaders in humanitarian action.

A PROFESSIONAL HUMANITARIAN ASSOCIATION: WHAT DOES IT LOOK LIKE?

Humanitarian action is a relatively new discipline. It needs to be built around providing the best care to beneficiaries and therefore should be based on a mechanism that builds accountability and the relevant skills, knowledge, tools, behaviours, and attitudes. It is unique in its multidisciplinary, multicontextual nature, which brings together people from different backgrounds, cultures, and countries. This makes using traditional definitions of, and frameworks for, professionalism difficult but not impossible. Thus, a modified concept of professionalization needs to be developed for the humanitarian sphere. The definition of professional in the humanitarian context should incorporate the notion of a "traditional professional" (such as a doctor or engineer) in addition to one who engages in humanitarian work as a full-time career but who is not university-trained. It should also embrace the diversity of the humanitarian community and consider experience as something that is just as valuable as is formal training and certification.

It also needs to recognize different training and educational programs from all organizations and countries around the world.
This raises several questions: What is the value of field experience? How does it compare to academic programming? Where
do non-university-based training programs (such as those offered
internally by the organizations themselves) come in? How do we
compare training across organizations and countries?

The value of experience cannot be overlooked. Currently, there
are over twenty-seven thousand MSF workers in over sixty countries worldwide, many of whom call themselves professional
humanitarians because they engage in humanitarian work full
time. They not only work on the ground in emergency settings
but also engage in innovative technologies, tools, and approaches
in order to meet the changing health needs of the populations
they serve. They attend MSF training sessions, meetings, confer-
ences, and debriefings. They write articles, conduct research, and
participate in active and relevant debates about the humanitarian
community and practice. Although the organization employs doctors, most of its human resources comprise national staff and
humanitarians who are not from the traditional professional
associations. Does this mean that they cannot be considered
professional humanitarians?

In order to include experience, training, and academic and
professional certification, a framework for professionalization
would have to have several levels. Peter Walker proposes that a
model for humanitarian professionalization might comprise three
tiers, such that it looks like an upside down triangle. The levels,
or tiers, would be:

TIER 1: Recognized professionals such as doctors and
engineers who also have competency in humanitarian action.
TIER 2: Master's-level or university training that provides a
certification in humanitarian action or a related discipline
(e.g., a master's in public health with a concentration in
humanitarian studies). Individuals from Tier 1 could also
be included here.

TIER 3: Humanitarians who are field experienced and/or who have taken professional development training courses such as those offered by RedR, Bioforce, Red Cross, MSF, or the UN (to cite a few). Individuals from tiers 1 and 2 could also be included in Tier 3.

The humanitarian community has been looking at models for professionalization that have been used by other associations. I briefly discuss three of these.

1 Mountain Leaders: The Mountain Leaders have had formal training since 1964. The entry-level five-day qualifying exam tests knowledge and skills in the field. Approximately seven thousand people take this exam each year, but only two hundred become certified. Progression to the top tier of Mountain Guide is for true experts who have years of experience and training. Only a handful of people achieve this level. The training is not standardized or competency based; however, the standard for certification is the same throughout the world. In other words, the individual process for training is unique but the end result, once one is considered a professional (which follows the "tiered" theme above), is the same.

2 Logistics and Transport: The Humanitarian and Emergency Logistics Professionals (HELP) started by mapping the logistics of a professional association. From there, it grew organically. Today there are three levels of certification, or "tiers," within the profession. Similar to the Mountain Leaders, how one gets to each level is an independent process, allowing for informal learning through in-company schemes. The certifying body for this association is independent and only provides the certification process.

3 Emergency Medicine in North America: Emergency medicine (EM) as a medical specialty is relatively young. EM was born as a specialty in order to fill the time commitment required by physicians on staff to work in the increasingly chaotic emergency departments. It was not until the establishment of

the American College of Emergency Physicians (ACEP); the
recognition of emergency medicine training programs by the
AMA (American Medical Association); and, in 1979, a historical vote by the American Board of Medical Specialties that
EM became a recognized medical specialty.[16] The model of
specialty recognition and professional development followed
a "top-down" approach, whereby an organization was
founded in order to organize and legitimize its members.

The three examples of professional associations indicate that
there are different ways to form a professional association. An
association can be created by a top-down strategy or by an organic,
bottom-up strategy that allows individuals to grow the organization organically. Professionals in Humanitarian Assistance and
Protection (PHAP) has grown its association by using the latter
strategy.[17] PHAP's community of professional humanitarians
functions like a cooperative: its members join for services and are
part of the evolving normative processes and strategies. Given the
diversity of the humanitarian community, PHAP may provide the
best model for a professional humanitarian association.

CORE COMPETENCIES

Core competencies form the basis for most professional degree
and many training programs. The Consortium of British Humanitarian Agencies (CBHA) is the first humanitarian organization to
build a "humanitarian competency framework" that includes a
learning and evaluation framework specific to humanitarian
training and field-craft. The CBHA was created to strengthen the
capacity of the NGO sector to deliver appropriate, high-quality,
and swift humanitarian assistance to populations affected by
disaster. It consists of fifteen UK-based NGOs that have committed
to implementing five objectives that support this purpose.[18] These
objectives are:

1 increasing access to fast, efficient, and effective funding for
   front-line humanitarian work;

2 increasing numbers of competent national and international managers and leaders;

3 increasing agency surge capacity to respond appropriately to new emergencies;

4 strengthening humanitarian logistics systems; and

5 learning and education.

The Core Humanitarian Competencies Framework developed by the CBHA consists of sixteen core competencies distributed among six categories and divided into two main sections: (1) core behaviours for all staff and (2) additional behaviours for first-level line managers. Most humanitarian stakeholders now recognize this framework as the standard for categorizing competencies. It is largely used for self-assessment but can also be used for hiring and for performance benchmarks. These competencies have recently been field-tested and will become the foundational competencies for the skills, knowledge, and attitudes – the hard and soft skills – that are required of a humanitarian professional. Although they are not meant for measuring academic performance, these competencies provide a model from which academic program competencies can evolve.

The Network of Humanitarian Assistance International Association of Universities, a thirty-university consortium that offers master's programs in humanitarian action, has also developed a list of competencies that fall under three headings:

- Vision: global and comprehensive vision of the humanitarian world.
- Personal integrity: capacity for self-management and to inspire and provide humanitarian strategic leadership.
- Strategic management: capacity to manage high impact organizations and complex humanitarian responses.

Core competencies for humanitarian education are required in order to create competent leaders of humanitarian action – to ensure that the requisite knowledge, skills, tools, attitudes, and behaviours are included in humanitarian training programs and that they can be adapted to many situations. Their purpose is to ensure that the needs of beneficiaries and organizations are met. Finally, they are key to standardizing the training that will lead to certification and professionalization.

CERTIFICATION

The issue of core curriculum and certification is heavily debated in the humanitarian community. Many practitioners associated with NGOs resist the idea of one certifying process and prefer self-assessment tools, whereas academics need more stringent criteria in order to satisfy their institutional requirements. In order to accommodate the many different NGO-based training programs, university degrees, and years of field experience, certification for humanitarian action will need to consider a non-conventional path. Humanitarian certification could apply the process used by Mountain Guides and grandfather in those who have had years of field experience. One way to respect the diversity of training processes in the humanitarian sector would be to create a certification passport that would enable all training to be entered into one book and that, when combined with experience, would amount to a tier within the professional framework. The passport would function as the principle document for humanitarian certification and would be recognized worldwide, even though the individual training may be country- or organization-based. Academic diplomas and degrees would also be included in the certification passport.

FUNCTIONS OF A PROFESSIONAL ASSOCIATION

A professional humanitarian association would have a number of functions. These would include career advice, job opportunities, and professional development activities (including training, education, internship, mentorship, and member support). A professional association would offer good communication and an exchange of training and information between NGO, academic, UN, and other groups that make up the humanitarian community.

It should also include a mechanism to allow for follow-up on issues pertaining to individual quality and accountability as well as recourse in cases of negligence or malpractice.

CONCLUSION AND RECOMMENDATIONS

There are many obstacles to developing a professional humanitarian framework. These include issues around lack of training standards, career paths, and partner capacity for staff training. There is so much diversity within the humanitarian community that consensus will be difficult. There is the danger of over-bureaucracy, prohibitive cost, lack of funding, and an endless paper chase (from individuals, organizations, and academic institutions to determining who will be responsible for it all). Policing and monitoring professional conduct in the field will be a contentious issue. Questions around voluntary versus compulsory membership will need to be answered. Finally, the value of experience as opposed to academic training, and what this means for certification, will need to be explored. These are only some of the hurdles that will need to be overcome as this process moves forward.

In conclusion, the purpose of creating a professional humanitarian association is to improve the experiences of beneficiaries through establishing standards and principles that will be adhered to by the profession's members. The process needs to respect the diversity and universality of the humanitarian community while supporting its individuals, keeping communication open, and moving ahead with open discussion and participation.

NOTES

1 The IASC is the United Nations' primary mechanism for inter-agency coordination of humanitarian assistance. See http://www.humanitarianinfo.org/iasc (viewed 1 June 2011).

2 World Health Organization, *Introducing a Competency Model for Public Health and Humanitarian Action*, draft discussion paper, version 1.0., 21 July 2011.

3 Sphere Project, *Sphere Handbook 2011*, ed. Phil Greaney, Sue Pfiffner, David Wilson, available at http://www.sphereproject.org (viewed 21 July 2011).

4 LEGS Project, "Livestock Emergency Guidelines and Standards," *Practical Action Publishing*, 2009, available at http://www.livestock-emergency.net (viewed 1 June 2011).

5 "HAP: Human Accountability Partnership" (Geneva: HAP International), available at http://www.hapinternational.org/ (viewed 1 June 2011).

6 "ALNAP: Active Learning Network for Accountability and Performance in Humanitarian Action" (London, ALNAP), available at http://www.alnap.org/ (viewed 1 June 2011).

7 "People in Aid" (London: People in Aid), available at http://www.peopleinaid.org/ (viewed 1 June 2011).

8 "The Good Enough Guide by the Emergency Capacity Building Project," available at http://www.ecbproject.org/GoodEnoughGuide (viewed 5 November 2011).

9 "The Compass Method by Groupe Urgence, Réhabilitation, Développement (URD)," available at http://www.compasqualite.org (viewed 22 September 2011).

10 Coordination Solidarité, Urgence, Développement (SUD), "The Synergie Qualité Guide 2005," available at http://www.coordinationsud.org (viewed 22 September 2011).

11 "The Inter-Agency Network for Education in Emergencies (INEE)," available at http://www.ineesite.org/ (viewed 22 September 2011).

12 P. Walker and C. Russ, *Professionalizing the Humanitarian Sector: A Scoping Study* (London: Enhancing Learning and Research for Humanitarian Assistance, 2010), available at http://www.elrha.org/uploads/Professionalising_the_humanitarian_sector.pdf (viewed 1 June 2011).

13 Presentation by Jean-Daniel Rainhorn, Humanitarian Education Conference, 25–27 October 2011, Geneva, Switzerland, available at http://www.humanitarianeducation.org/ (viewed April 2012) and http://www.cerahgeneve.ch/ (viewed April 2012).

14 Enhancing Learning and Research for Humanitarian Assistance, *Survey on Humanitarian Professionalism*, results presented at the Humanitarian Education Conference, 25–27 October 2011, Geneva,

Switzerland, available at http://www.humanitarianeducation.org/, http://www.elrha.org/.

15 "Network on Humanitarian Assistance (NOHA)," available at http://www.nohanet.org/ (viewed 5 November 2011).

16 "Emergency Medicine," available at http://en.wikipedia.org/wiki/ Emergency_medicine – cite_note-1 (viewed 5 November 2011).

17 "Professionals in Humanitarian Assistance and Protection," available at http://www.phapinternational.org/ (viewed 5 November 2011).

18 B. Emmens and S. Swords, CBHA Humanitarian Capacity Building Program: Objective 1 Final Report (London, UK: 10 August 2010), available at http://www.ecbproject.org/resources/library/90-cbha-humanitarian-capacity-building-program-objective-1-final-report (viewed 5 November 2011).

Conclusion:
The Shape of Things to Come –
An Essay on Humanitarian Challenges

PETER WALKER

INTRODUCTION

The past decade has seen a rash of major complicated disasters: the 2004 Asia tsunami, an earthquake in Haiti, floods in Pakistan, a tsunami in Japan, and drought and famine in the Horn of Africa. A complex combination of climate change, globalization, and the breakdown of any semblance of good governance seems to have tipped communities from survival into destitution. What is going on? A statistical anomaly or a glimpse of things to come? In this chapter I seek to put these recent crises into context by looking at the role climate change and globalization are playing in driving disasters. I then reflect on what this means for how humanitarian agencies, and governments, need to respond.

CLIMATE CHANGE

Fortunately, we have a great laboratory in which to see how climate change affects human society: it is called history. Human history is peppered by periods of rapid climate change. If we go back to the middle Holocene (7000 BCE to 5500 BCE), records laid down in the sediments of the rivers flowing out of today's

Sahara show that over fifty-seven hundred years ago this was a fertile place. Then something changed: the rivers dried up, the savannah turned to marginal land, and the only places left habitable were the valleys where groundwater came to the surface to form oases. This rapid change took place over a period of about seven hundred years and was the engine behind a major change in society – away from a hunter-gatherer and pastoralist existence to a more concentrated urban existence in oasis settlements. It also led to shorter and more violent lives, to a more authoritarian form of government, and to the first land disputes in the Sahel.

Fast forward to 400 CE and we find the breakup of the Roman Empire coinciding with another period of rapid climate change, forcing mass migrations across Europe: Goths, Visigoths, and Vandals, all on the move in search of survival. Take another step forward to the beginnings of the Little Ice Age in Europe, around 1570, and a twenty-year period of systematic decline in temperature. Crop yields plummeted or failed, throwing this agrarian economy into rapid decline. Analysis of parish and court records shows an absolute correlation between the change in climate and rise in crime and violence across the continent.

And, finally, recent economic research in the Sahel, still dominated by agrarian communities, shows that, in a year of bad rainfall, GDP, which is driven by agriculture, tends to fall by maybe 5 percent, and that, for every 5 percent fall in GDP, the probability of marked civil unrest goes up by 50 percent.[1]

The message is clear: society does not cope well with stress, particularly stress applied at a pace to which it cannot adapt. When stress outpaces social adaptation, things break.

And, by the way, the pace of climate change, in all these historical periods, was never more that 50 percent of the pace of change today.

GLOBALIZATION

We know we are entering a period of rapid climate change, but that is not the only change hitting us. The globalizing of our economy is unleashing major economic, social, and political change, and we are struggling to bring our human adaptation up to speed. Globalization is creating tremendous wealth. The rise in living standards in Southeast Asia is something that, a generation ago, many of us only dreamed could occur. The political rise of China, to the point at which it is now the world's number two economy and the biggest investor in Africa, would have stunned the political pundits of the 1970s. The ability of mobile phone technology and social networking media to allow remote African villages to have banking facilities and to become part of the global credit culture, or the use of Facebook, LinkedIn, and Google maps to plan and execute peaceful revolutions in Georgia, Tunisia, or Egypt, seem like the plot of a sci-fi movie. All great stuff, but it has its dark side. It is also driving the most rapid increase ever in wealth disparities, to a point at which disparities in the United States and China now outshine those of the Roman Empire, the Ottoman Empire, and nineteenth-century Britain. It is a gravy train that seemingly comes as a package – all or nothing: and that "all" embraces the free market economy, consumerism, scientific positivism, and a squeamishness towards religion (unless it supports the greater objective of the free market).

Those disparities and exclusions, coupled with a sense, for those at the bottom of the economic miracle, that they are either left behind or not in control of their destinies, fuels violence and discontent. In its most extreme form it pushes whole cultures to feel abandoned and discriminated against.

ADAPTATION

And here is the concern: if we were only facing a near future of rapid climate change, that would be worrying enough, but this change is taking place at the same time as is globalization. Our global society is riding two roller coasters, and we control neither of them. So here is the key question: what can we do to help human society adapt quickly enough to absorb the stresses of change – stresses we cannot predict?

Well, one way we try to adsorb these stresses is through curtailing their worst excesses. That, in effect, is what humanitarian assistance does. It does not seek to change anything, just patch things up and keep people alive in extremis. But there are signs that this safeguard of last resort is also under stress.

WHEN IS RELIEF NOT RELIEF?

Humanitarian assistance is supposed to be a short-term measure, an exceptional response to an exceptional set of circumstances. It provides life-preserving aid to keep crisis victims going while a more durable solution is found for their plight. But what if no durable solution is being sought? Figures recently compiled by Development Initiatives, a UK-based group that tracks aid spending, show that today a full 70 percent of all humanitarian aid is spent on programs that have been running for at least five years and that 40 percent is going to programs that have been running for more than eight years. Furthermore, 60 percent of all humanitarian aid goes to countries with ongoing protracted conflicts.[2]

This is not quick-in quick-out emergency assistance. Humanitarian aid is shifting from being an emergency service to being a safety-net service. And when we look at where this funding is going – into Sudan, Somalia, Afghanistan, and Ethiopia – there is no evidence of there being a broad system in place that is seeking those durable solutions. In effect, humanitarian aid is holding people in limbo – or is it purgatory – keeping them alive but offering them no hope for the future.

AND THE FUTURE?

So where does this take us, with the probability of crises fuelled by climate change and globalization becoming more frequent, and the mechanisms of humanitarian aid being morphed into palliatives (keeping people from dying, yes, but maybe also locking in a false social stability, thus holding back much needed social and political adaptation)? Consider that recent reappraisals of the role of aid, principally Jointchurchaid in the Biafra conflict of the late 1960s, suggest that relief intervention, far from saving lives, actively prolonged the war by eighteen months, contributed to the deaths of 180,000 people, and allowed Nigeria and the UK to seek a "humanitarian" solution to Biafra rather than a political one.[3]

So where does this take us? What do we need to do differently in the future? I would offer the following suggestions.

First, we – agencies and states – need to change our perception of crises. In the future crisis will be normal, not exceptional. Expect the unexpected. This implies that crisis response should become part of the normal business of government (as it is in Bangladesh today). It means seeing international assistance as a normal part of the sovereign relations between states, not as a sign of weakness or the acceptance of charity. The attempts by the IFRC and the Red Crescent Societies to draft, and to help states enact, template national disaster response legislation marks an interesting move in this direction.

Second, crisis responders need to accept the consequences of their increased global role. Principally, this means creating and applying much more rigorous standards of competence to agencies and agency individuals. If a global system of crisis response is going to be the norm, then agencies seeking global accreditation for their competence will follow, as will the need for individuals to see themselves as part of a profession, with all that implies for individual competence, certification, and standards of professional conduct.

Finally, and this is maybe the most difficult question, can we continue to sustain the moral ambiguity of knowingly being part of a system that keeps people alive but offers them no chance of a better future? Do we need a new, maybe an additional, form of work? One that involves neither the highly limited, impartial, neutral, and lifesaving humanities aid nor the plodding holistic development program but, rather, some more agile form of aid that both seeks to sustain life in crises and seeks to offer opportunities for adaptation – adaptation of economies, society, and political structure?

The great thing about the future is that nothing is certain, particularly in economics and politics. Aid agencies can choose to carry on, business as normal, and I dare say they will prosper financially. Or they can choose to play an innovative role in helping society adapt to the new world ahead. The latter is a riskier course, certainly; however, humanitarianism's greatest successes have all occurred when we have taken risks and had the courage to run with them.

NOTES

1 M. Edward, S. Shanker, and E. Sergenti. "Economic Shocks and Civil Conflict: An Instrumental Variables Approach," *Journal of Political Economy* 112, 4 (2004): 725–53.

2 "Development Initiatives," *Global Humanitarian Assistance Report* (2009), 4, available at http://www.globalhumanitarianassistance.org/wp-content/uploads/2009/07/GHA-Report-2009.pdf (viewed April 2012).

3 John J. Stremlau, *The International Politics of the Nigerian Civil War* (Princeton, NJ: Princeton University Press, 1977), 240.

MSF Charter

Médecins Sans Frontières is a private, international association. The association is made up mainly of doctors and health sector workers and is also open to all other professions which might help in achieving its aims. All of its members agree to honour the following principles:

Médecins Sans Frontières provides assistance to populations in distress, to victims of natural or man-made disasters and to victims of armed conflict. They do so irrespective of race, religion, creed or political convictions.

Médecins Sans Frontières observes neutrality and impartiality in the name of universal medical ethics and the right to humanitarian assistance and claims full and unhindered freedom in the exercise of its functions.

Members undertake to respect their professional code of ethics and maintain complete independence from all political, economic or religious powers.

As volunteers, members understand the risks and dangers of the missions they carry out and make no claim for themselves or their assigns for any form of compensation other than that which the association might be able to afford them.

Contributors

CAROLINE ABU-SADA is the research unit director of MSF Switzerland. Holder of a political science and international relations PhD from Sciences Po Paris and an Arabic language degree from La Sorbonne, Abu-Sada has held several positions in the field, noticeably in the Middle East, for Oxfam GB, the United Nations Food and Agriculture Organization, and MSF Switzerland. Since 2010, she has represented MSF at the Steering Committee of the Centre for Studies and Research on Humanitarian Action in Geneva, a centre led by both the Graduate Institute and the University of Geneva. She also coordinates the Research Unit of MSF. She is the author of ONG *palestiniennes et construction étatique: L'expérience de Palestinian Agricultural Relief Committees (PARC) dans les Territoires occupés palestiniens, 1983–2005* (Beirut: IFPO, 2007); *Perception de MSF et de l'action humanitaire* (Lausanne: Editions Antipodes, 2011); *Le développement, une affaire d'ONG? Associations, Etats et Bailleurs dans le monde arabe* (Paris: Karthala-IREMAM-IFPO, 2012); as well as several articles, reports, and chapters on humanitarian action, NGOs, and the Middle East. She also taught political science at New York University in Paris and Sciences Po Lille (2001–06).

NAOMI ADELSON is associate professor, Department of Anthropology, York University, Toronto. She has a PhD from McGill University, Department of Anthropology; and an MA from

McMaster University, Department of Anthropology. Dr Adelson's main research interest is in medical anthropology and the anthropology of the body, focusing in particular on various aspects of the human/machine interface, including the Visible Human Project, the concept of the self in the age of genomics, and First Nations e-health in relation to identity and concepts of care. Her current work includes Webs of Health: An Ethnographic Study of the Interface between Internet Technologies, Health, and Identity of First Nations Women (a SSHRC Northern Research Development Program-funded project), and she recently hosted a CIHR-funded national interdisciplinary workshop on this topic entitled "Contextualizing Health Information Communication Technologies." She is a co-investigator with the National Network for Aboriginal Mental Health Research, a CIHR Network Environments for Aboriginal Health Research and with the CIHR-funded Ethics in Conditions of Disaster and Deprivation: Learning from Health Workers' Narratives research team.

DONALD COLE MD, MSc, FRCP(C) trained as a physician at the University of Toronto (1978). He then practised primary care, public health, occupational health, and environmental health in a variety of settings in Canada and lower- and middle-income countries. In a community medicine residency at McMaster University he completed a master's in design, measurement and evaluation of health services (1991) and went on to qualify as a Royal College fellow in occupational medicine (1990) and community medicine (1992). He developed a long-standing relationship with the International Potato Center around agriculture and health research for development, with a particular focus on pesticides, urban agriculture, and nutrition. A Tri-Council Eco-Research fellowship in environmental epidemiology and the role of interim director of research followed by senior scientist at the Institute for Work and Health fostered a focus on research. As a tenured associate professor and interim head of the Global Health Division at the Dalla Lana School of Public Health at the University of Toronto, he currently teaches, mentors, and contributes research evidence to public health practice and policy, with a developing interest in global health research capacity development evaluation. He is director of the Collaborative PhD Program in Global Health and co-chairs the Capacity Development Program area of the Canadian Coalition for Global Health Research.

FRANÇOIS COOREN (PhD, University of Montreal) is professor and chair of the Department of Communication at the University of Montreal. He authored two books published by John Benjamins (*The Organizing Property of Communication*, 2000; *Action and Agency in Dialogue*, 2010) as well as close to forty peer-reviewed articles published in international journals and twenty book chapters. He was the editor-in chief of *Communication Theory* from 2005 to 2008 and edited two books published by Lawrence Erlbaum (*Communication as Organizing*, 2006; *Interacting and Organizing*, 2007). His research interests lie in the study of organizational communication, language, and social interaction; and communication theory. He is past president of the International Communication Association (2010–11), an academic association that counts close to forty-five hundred members coming from eighty-five countries around the world.

LAURIE ELIT (MD, MSc, FRCPS) is an associate professor in the Department of Obstetrics and Gynaecology at McMaster University, Hamilton, Ontario; and in the Department of Oncology and General Surgery, McMaster University Department of Obstretrics and Gynaecology, University of Toronto. She is a member of the Division of Gynecologic Oncology at the Juravinski Cancer Centre in Hamilton, Ontario. She is a member of the executive of the gynecological disease site group for the National Cancer Institute Canada, and the Program in Evidence-Based Medicine for Cancer Care Ontario. Her clinical and research interests involve a variety of women's health issues, such as health services research and treatment decision making in ovarian cancer and the management of CIN 1 Cervical Intraepithelial Neoplasia 1 (abnormal cervical cell growth).

LARISSA FAST earned her PhD (2002) from the Institute for Conflict Analysis and Resolution (ICAR) at George Mason University in Fairfax, Virginia. Her research focuses primarily on violence

against aid workers and aid agencies, and she has completed a
book manuscript entitled Aid in Danger. Other research interests
include humanitarian politics, development and conflict, evaluation, and peacebuilding. She has worked for international organizations, primarily in North America and Africa, as a project
manager, consultant, and trainer. Fast's recent and forthcoming
publications include a chapter on violence against aid workers in
the European Journal of International Relations (2010), a chapter
on tensions between humanitarian relief and peacebuilding in
Strategies of Peace (Oxford: Oxford University Press, 2010),
articles on NGO security (Disasters, August 2007), and she has
co-authored articles on the acceptance approach to security management (forthcoming in Disasters) and on evaluation and peacebuilding (Journal of Peacebuilding and Development, 2005). She
was co-editor, with Sandra Cheldelin and Daniel Druckmam, of
a textbook on conflict resolution entitled *Conflict: From Analysis
to Intervention* 2nd ed. (New York: Continuum, 2008).

MATTHEW HUNT (PT, PhD) is an assistant professor in the School
of Physical and Occupational Therapy, affiliate member of the
Biomedical Ethics Unit, and associate member of the Division of
Experimental Medicine, all at McGill University, Montreal. He
chairs the Clinical Ethics Committee of the Shriners Hospital for
Children in Montreal. Previously, he has worked as a physio-
therapist in Montreal, the Canadian Arctic, North Africa, and the
Balkans. Matthew conducts research that addresses ethical issues
related to two domains: (1) global health engagement and (2) rehabilitation care and professions. In the area of global health ethics
he is currently pursuing research related to ethics of humanitarian
assistance and development work, international clinical electives
for students of the health professions, and the conduct of global
public health research.

KIRSTEN JOHNSON is an assistant professor in the Faculty of
Medicine, associate faculty at the Institute for Health and Social
Policy, and the founding director of the Humanitarian Studies
Initiative at McGill University in Montreal. She is one of the
founding members of the Harvard Humanitarian Initiative at

Harvard University in Boston, where she is affiliate faculty, teaching humanitarian studies. Dr Johnson is a partner in the Humanitarian Training Initiative, an organization that partners with the World Health Organization, among others, to provide predeployment training; a Steering Committee member of the Child Soldiers Initiative; and a board member of the International Humanitarian Studies Association. Dr Johnson's research focuses on genocide, child combatants, sexual gender-based violence, and conflict-related mental health and psychosocial support. She has been involved in humanitarian professionalization, working – as part of Enhancing Learning and Research for Humanitarian Assistance – on the development of competencies for training, education, and certification in this sector. She was awarded the Segal Centre's 2010 Januscz Korczak Award for her work on protecting the rights of children in conflict, the College of Family Physicians of Canada Award of Excellence for contributions to International Health and Humanitarian Assistance in 2010, and Canada's Top 40 Under 40 for 2011.

KHURSHIDA MAMBETOVA started her professional carrier at UNESCO in 1998. She was actively engaged in ensuring the financial sustainability and management of UNESCO projects aimed at safeguarding intangible cultural heritage. Since 2002, Khurshida has worked several years at the ICRC. She was primarily engaged in the organizational development of National Red Crescent Societies in Central Asia. Then, as the ICRC delegate and head of office, she implemented programs that involved protecting civilians affected by conflicts in South Ossetia and Nagorny-Karabakh, visiting places of detention, distributing food, and supplying water for displaced persons and refugees. For the past year, Khurshida participated in the MSF perception research supported by MSF Canada (field visits to Chad and Kyrgyzstan) and organized the MSF conference on perception of humanitarian action in Montreal.

FRÉDÉRIK MATTE has a BA and an MSc from the University of Montreal, where he is a doctoral candidate. He worked for several years in corporate communications and in politics, and for the past five years he has been involved with MSF as a communication officer.

JOHN PRINGLE is a registered nurse and epidemiologist, with a BScN from McMaster University in Hamilton and an MSc in community health and epidemiology from Queen's University in Kingston. He worked as a northern outpost nurse in remote First Nations communities before joining MSF in 2001, when he helped provide primary health care in refugee camps along the Eritrean-Ethiopian border. In 2006, he conducted his second mission with MSF, investigating outbreaks of meningitis across northern Nigeria, and in 2010 he returned to northern Nigeria with an MSF emergency team to respond to mass lead poisoning outbreaks in rural villages. He is currently a PhD candidate in the Dalla Lana School of Public Health and the Joint Centre for Bioethics at the University of Toronto. His research focuses on the application of global health ethics to humanitarian and public health emergencies.

LYNDA REDWOOD-CAMPBELL has research and scholarly interests in the areas of immigrant/refugee health and global health. After completing her medical degree (1992) and residency, she earned a diploma in tropical medicine and hygiene from the London School of Tropical Medicine and Hygiene, United Kingdom. She also completed her master's in public health (international health) at Johns Hopkins Bloomberg School of Public Health and was elected to the Delta Omega Honorary Society in the United States. Dr Redwood-Campbell has worked in many resource-poor countries. Some examples include Indonesia, Rwanda, the Democratic Republic of Congo, Kenya, Honduras, and Bangladesh. She worked with the ICRC Red Cross field hospital in Banda Aceh, Indonesia, after the December 2004 tsunami. She also conducted relief work in November 2005 after the Kashmir earthquake in Pakistan. She is now working with the University of Syiah Kuala and the Rotary Clubs to build capacity in health personnel resources in Banda Aceh, Indonesia. Her research includes immigrant women's barriers to cervical cancer screening, the health of the Kosovars, the health of immigrants in Canada, HIV/AIDS in the Caribbean, and the health issues of post-tsunami survivors. She is chair of the International (Global) Health Committee at the Canadian College of Family Physicians; is on the International Advisory Committee of the World Association of Disaster and Emergency Medicine; and is a board member of the International Women and Children's Network, McMaster University. Dr Redwood-Campbell has been a consultant to the WHO, Health Action in Crisis cluster in 2008–09. Her interest is in how to integrate primary health care (including equity and social justice concepts) into disaster preparedness and response in policy and in reality, particularly in low-income countries (where the most vulnerable are most affected). Dr Redwood-Campbell has a clinical practice at McMaster University at the West End Clinic in Hamilton, Ontario, where she teaches and provides a range of primary care services.

LISA SCHWARTZ is the Arnold L. Johnson Chair in Health Care Ethics in the Faculty of Health Sciences at McMaster University, associate professor in the Department of Clinical Epidemiology and Biostatistics, associate director of the Centre for Health Economics and Policy Analysis, and associate member of the Department of Philosophy. Dr Schwartz teaches for the DeGroote School of Medicine, the Bachelor of Health Sciences Programme, in Health Research Methodologies and has a PhD in health policy. She is the primary investigator on a CIHR-funded study examining the ethical challenges faced by health care professionals providing humanitarian health care assistance abroad. She is also a co-PI on a related study of professional ethics and role conflicts for health care professionals working in military and humanitarian contexts.

CHRIS SINDING is an associate professor in the Department of Health, Aging and Society, School of Social Work, Kenneth Taylor Hall, McMaster University, Hamilton, Ontario. She has a PhD from the Social Science and Health Program, Department of Public Health Sciences, University of Toronto; and an MA, Social

Welfare Policy, School of Social Work, McMaster University.
Dr Sinding is interested in women's health and health care, particularly women's experiences of breast cancer and gynaecological cancer; community-based cancer activism, care, and support;
the interface between formal and informal care, especially end-
of-life care; and innovative research representation/knowledge
exchange, particularly research-based theatre. Her current
research examines the social organization of cancer care and
interactions between providers and patients to better understand
who gets what and why (especially focusing on class privilege and
disadvantage). With an interdisciplinary research team, Dr Sinding is currently conducting a study examining the social organization of cancer care, focusing on the significance of social class,
age, and "race." A second study explores the ethical challenges
described by Canadian-trained health professionals who have
provided care through humanitarian agencies (PI Lisa Schwartz),
especially respondents' accounts of allocating care in contexts of
resource scarcity.

PETER WALKER was appointed, in September 2002, as the
director of the Feinstein International Center at Tufts University,
Boston, Massachusetts, after twenty-five years of fieldwork in
response to various humanitarian crises around the world. In
2007, Dr Walker was made Rosenberg Professor of Nutrition and
Human Security. He played a major role in managing the relief
response to the 1984–85 famine in Sudan and in subsequent relief
and development programs in Ethiopia. Joining the IFRC and Red
Crescent Societies in 1990, Dr Walker was involved in needs
assessment and evaluation missions in the former Soviet states,
Iran, Pakistan, the former Yugoslavia, the Horn of Africa,
Namibia, Malawi, Somalia, and the Great Lakes region. He
developed the global Code of Conduct for disaster relief workers
and steered the Sphere Project, a major NGO and UN collaborative
effort to develop universal competence standards of humanitarian
assistance. In 1993, Dr Walker founded the annual *World Disasters Report*, which has now become a standard reference text in
the humanitarian business. His recent book, written with Feinstein

Center faculty member Dr Dan Maxwell, *Shaping the Humanitarian World*, provides a robust history of humanitarianism linked to an inquiry into its future as a global venture. At the Feinstein Intentional Center Dr Walker is actively involved in research examining the future global drivers of humanitarian crises, the effectiveness of international humanitarian systems, and the creation of international accreditation systems for professionals.

Index

academia/academic/academics, 4, 7, 12, 104, 106, 107, 108, 111, 112, 113, 127

acceptance, 6, 45, 80, 90–103, 120, 128

accountability, 6, 98, 102, 105, 107, 113, 114

adherence, 11, 14, 19, 105

Afghanistan, 89, 93, 94, 97, 102, 103, 119

agenda, 58, 74, 80, 83, 89; hidden, 12; humanitarian, 12; political, 3, 15

aid workers, 6, 7, 27, 35, 50, 62, 63, 74, 78, 89, 90, 99, 128

armed: conflict, 3, 5, 123; escort, 24, 90, 101; forces, 13 guard, 94

arrogance, 41

attitudes, 19, 24, 36, 44, 79, 86, 92, 107, 111

authorities, 5, 12, 13, 18, 19, 22, 24, 26, 27, 35, 36, 37, 40, 44, 46, 90, 91, 117

behaviour, 34, 54, 55, 75, 93, 95, 99, 100, 107, 111

beneficiaries, 6, 18, 62, 90, 91, 94, 97, 100, 107, 112, 113

Biafra, 4, 119, 120

biomedical, 53, 55, 128

Cameroon, 16

challenges, 1, 3, 4, 5, 7, 12, 13, 15, 17, 21, 26, 40, 48, 65, 68, 71, 79, 86, 91, 96, 105, 116; ethical, 6, 49, 73, 74, 77, 80, 81, 83, 84, 85, 131, 132

chelation therapy, 48, 50, 60

China, 118

climate change, 105, 116, 117, 118, 119

collaboration, 11, 18, 22, 23, 31

communication, 4, 5, 6, 17, 20, 21, 22, 23, 24, 26, 30, 32, 33, 34, 46, 47, 49, 56, 60, 93, 104, 112, 113, 126, 127, 129, 130

conflict, 3, 5, 27, 28, 67, 73, 76, 77, 84, 87, 94, 105, 119, 121, 123, 127, 128, 129, 131

Context, 4, 12, 13, 15, 17, 21, 27,
    30, 31, 40, 45, 49, 50, 51, 58,
    60, 62, 63, 73, 74, 76, 77, 83,
    91, 92, 93, 104, 116, 126, 132;
    cultural, 75, 94, 95; economic,
    54; given, 16, 85; historical,
    55, 56; humanitarian, 107,
    131; local, 20, 84; political, 5,
    14; social, 55, 79, 80
cooperation, 26, 34, 35, 43, 44,
    45, 63
crisis, 27, 58, 66, 119, 131; Darfur,
    23; financial, 49, 57, 63; hu-
    manitarian, 104; system of, 120

dilemmas, 4, 6, 68, 69, 87
Doctors Without Borders. See
    Médecins Sans Frontières

emergency, 5, 14, 32, 48, 50, 58,
    59, 60, 61, 62, 63, 66, 87, 105,
    108, 109, 110, 114, 115, 119,
    130, 131
epidemics, 3, 48, 49, 50, 51, 52,
    53, 54, 55, 57, 58, 59, 60, 61,
    62, 63, 65, 68
exclusion, 3, 118
expatriates, 6, 12, 18, 21, 25, 80,
    83, 88, 94, 100
experience (professional), 25, 30,
    34, 35, 37, 38, 39, 45, 50, 62,
    73, 75, 77, 84, 85, 88, 91, 95,
    104, 105, 106, 107, 108, 109,
    112

field (humanitarian), 4, 5, 6, 11, 12,
    13, 14, 15, 16, 31, 35, 36, 37,

38, 39, 40, 43, 44, 46, 50, 53,
    59, 60, 61, 73, 74, 77, 79, 81,
    82, 84, 85, 96, 102, 103, 104,
    105, 106, 107, 108, 109, 110,
    111, 112, 113, 125, 130, 132
figures, 6, 30, 32, 33, 34, 35, 36,
    37, 38, 39, 40, 41, 42, 43, 45,
    46, 47, 64, 119
footprint (of NGOs), 89, 98, 101

globalization, 48, 49, 56, 57, 58,
    59, 60, 62, 63, 67, 68, 116,
    117, 118, 119
governance, 116
Guatemala, 16
Gulf, 16

Haiti, 14, 104, 105, 116
headquarter, 6, 15, 31, 35, 36, 37,
    40, 79
health care, 3, 6, 56, 57, 58, 60,
    63, 65, 67, 73, 74, 75, 76, 77,
    80, 83, 84, 85, 86, 87, 88, 130,
    131, 132
host: community, 11, 83;
    country, 16, 41; culture, 80;
    governments, 94
humanitarian: action, 1, 3, 4, 6, 7,
    11, 12, 15, 32, 33, 59, 67, 84,
    85, 87, 104, 105, 106, 107,
    108, 111, 112, 113, 114, 125,
    129; aid, 6, 19, 26, 58, 60, 62,
    63, 68, 76, 84, 86; space, 16,
    23, 27, 28

identity, 4, 11, 16, 29, 43, 74, 95,
    126

innovative, 21, 100, 108, 121, 132
institution, 6, 7, 12, 13, 16, 19, 20,
    22, 24, 26, 56, 58, 63, 112, 113
instrumentalization, 45, 100
Iraq, 13, 15

leaders, 18, 21, 91, 94, 97, 98,
    106, 107, 109, 111
lead-poisoning, 5, 48, 50, 55, 57,
    58, 59, 60, 61, 62, 63
legitimacy, 32, 106

Médecins Sans Frontières, 4, 5, 6,
    7, 8, 9, 11, 12, 13, 14, 15, 16,
    17, 18, 19, 20, 21, 22, 23, 24,
    25, 26, 27, 30, 31, 32, 33, 34,
    35, 37, 38, 40, 41, 42, 43, 44,
    45, 46, 47, 48, 50, 53, 59, 60,
    61, 62, 63, 64, 68, 69, 74, 77,
    87, 108, 109, 123, 125, 129,
    130
medical: activity, 16, 17; assis-
    tance, 3, 5, 32; relief, 3
mining sector, 48, 50, 52, 53, 54,
    55, 61, 63, 66
MSF. See Médecins Sans Frontières
MSF-CH. See Médecins Sans
    Frontières

natural disaster, 3, 81
neoliberal, 48, 49, 56, 57, 59, 61,
    62, 63, 67, 68
neoliberalism, 56, 57, 67, 68
Niger, 13, 16, 31, 52, 54
Nigeria, 39, 48, 49, 50, 51, 52,
    55, 557, 58, 59, 61, 62, 63, 64,
    65, 66, 67, 68, 120, 121, 130

norm, 74, 79, 80, 81, 82, 83, 85,
    110, 120

Occupied Palestinian territories,
    15; Gaza, 15
oil, 27, 51, 53, 54, 57, 64, 69

patient, 11, 14, 17, 18, 20, 21, 25,
    30, 32, 35, 39, 41, 42, 43, 44,
    60, 62, 75, 76, 80, 81, 82, 83,
    84, 86, 132
perception, 3, 5, 6, 8, 9, 11, 12,
    13, 15, 16, 17, 18, 19, 20, 22,
    23, 24, 26, 27, 29, 30, 33, 34,
    45, 46, 71, 84, 87, 89, 90, 91,
    92, 94, 96, 97, 98, 99, 101,
    120, 125, 129; gap, 13, 26,
    97, 98
poverty, 48, 49, 50, 51, 52, 55,
    56, 58, 63, 65, 66, 72, 105
priority/priorities, 4, 51, 57, 58,
    75, 76, 84
proximity, 16, 35, 41, 42, 43, 44,
    45, 46
public health, 49, 50, 54, 55, 57,
    58, 59, 62, 63, 66, 67, 68, 76,
    87, 107, 108, 113, 126, 128,
    130, 131

quality of care, 25, 35, 42

recognition, 25, 29, 106, 110
Red Crescent Societies, 66, 87,
    120, 129, 132
Red Cross, 4, 66, 85, 87, 109, 130
refugee, 19, 20, 102, 129; camp,
    40, 42, 130

relationship, 89, 90, 91, 92, 93, 94, 95, 99, 100, 126
representation/misrepresentation, 26, 34, 102, 132
research, 4, 5, 6, 11, 12, 13, 14, 15, 16, 17, 18, 27, 30, 31, 33, 46, 53, 61, 86, 90, 95, 97, 99, 100, 102, 103, 106, 108, 114, 117, 125, 126, 127, 128, 129, 130, 131, 132, 133
responsibility, 3, 36, 58, 59, 60, 76, 83, 99

scarcity, 74, 77, 132
security, 6, 14, 15, 16, 19, 20, 21, 23, 24, 35, 39, 40, 41, 42, 44, 57, 62, 63, 69, 74, 84, 89, 90, 91, 92, 93, 94, 95, 96, 97, 98, 99, 101, 102, 103, 128, 132
skills, 27, 45, 56, 94, 107, 109, 111
South Sudan, 90, 93, 94, 95, 96, 97, 98, 99, 101, 102, 103
Sphere Project, 85, 87, 105, 107, 114, 132
staff, 6, 12, 14, 15, 16, 17, 18, 19, 21, 25, 26, 35, 38, 40, 60, 89, 90, 93, 94, 95, 96, 98, 99, 100, 101, 105, 106, 108, 111, 113
stakeholders, 5, 11, 12, 18, 20, 90, 91, 92, 93, 94, 95, 96, 97, 99, 100, 111
standard, 26, 30, 31, 33, 75, 85, 86, 105, 107, 109, 111, 112, 113, 114, 118, 120, 132
strategy/strategies, 28, 36, 37, 59, 62, 68, 96, 105, 110,

128; acceptance, 91, 93, 95, 97; communication 5, 20; humanitarian, 111; institutional, 22; management, 90, 111
students, 4, 7, 12, 13, 18, 27, 88, 107, 128
study/studies, 11, 12, 14, 15, 16, 17, 18, 20, 21, 22, 23, 26, 27, 29, 30, 69, 73, 74, 75, 77, 86, 106, 108, 114, 125, 126, 127, 128, 129, 131, 132
Sudan, 16, 17, 39, 94, 95, 119, 132

Témoignage, 4, 7, 16, 63, 69; speaking out, 15, 62; witnessing, 15, 49
tension, 25, 30, 34, 35, 42, 43, 44, 45, 77, 128
training, 17, 18, 22, 25, 26, 30, 45, 74, 75, 76, 77, 84, 85, 86, 104, 105, 106, 108, 109, 110, 111, 112, 113, 129

university, 6, 18, 45, 67, 86, 87, 106, 107, 108, 111, 112, 121, 125, 126, 127, 128, 129, 130, 131, 132

ventriloquism, 30, 32, 33, 47
video, 31, 35

withdrawal (of mission), 39, 59, 76, 90